The Complete Guide to
Dwarf Seahorses
in the Aquarium

Dedication

For my wonderful family, husband Mark, and two sons, Justin and Ian. You keep me always going strong. To Pete Giwojna, I could never have done this without you.

Acknowledgements

The author would like to acknowledge the following individuals for their contributions: Pete Giwojna, May and Heather Abbott, Charles and Maria Wagner, Robert Brown, Craig and Carol Cozzi-Smarr of Ocean Rider, all of you at Reefcentral and syngnathids.org, Tracey and Tim Steelman of Propagation, Inc., and finally my dear friend Lesslie Leddo who provided many photos for the book on such short notice.

T.F.H. Publications
One TFH Plaza
Third and Union Avenues
Neptune City, NJ 07753
www.tfh.com

ISBN 0-7938-0534-1

Distributed by T.F.H. Publications, Inc.

The Author wishes to thank the following photographers for their work on this book: Steve Buck, 135; O.M. Clark, 85; J. Kelly Giwojna, 16; Tari Kovets, 11, 13,19, 31, 39, 55, 67, 91, 113; Aaron Norman, 127; Mark Smith, 131, 134; Tracey Steelman, 94, 95, 107; Dr. Clyde Tamaru, 130, 121; Tracy Warland, 137; and Kyle Walcza, 138.

All other photos courtesy of Leslie Leddo's Limited Editions, Leslie Leddo, Photographer.

Front cover photo by J. Kelly Giwojna and back cover photos by Leslie Leddo.

Book design by Candida Moreira Tómassini.

The Complete Guide to
Dwarf Seahorses
in the Aquarium

Alisa Wagner Abbott

Table of Contents

Foreword

When I read this manuscript, I discovered I share something in common with the author. Like Alisa Abbott, dwarves were my first love out of all the seahorses. Like her, my first specimens were mail-order ponies shipped directly to me from a collector in Florida. In my case, it was decades ago, and I ordered my dwarf seahorses from a tiny ad in the back of a magazine, rather than through the Internet. Just like the directions that came with Alisa's kit many years later, the care instructions I received with my kit were woefully inadequate and my first ponies suffered as a result.

My first impression of Alisa's book was thus that it's about time—a manual like this will save future dwarf seahorse keepers a world of grief and spare their pets a lot of needless suffering. As I poured over the manuscript, I couldn't help thinking, "Boy, if only a guidebook like this had been available back then."

Like so many others, what first attracted me to dwarf seahorses was a chance to keep a legendary creature whose many fantastic features made it seem more like something out of a Disney movie than a living, breathing animal. Who wouldn't be fascinated by a bizarre beast that combined a horse's head with a monkey's grasping tail, the turreted eyes of a lizard, the armor plating of an armadillo, and an amazing color-changing ability that would turn a chameleon green with envy? Who could resist the antics of such an amazing oddity—a fish that has a neck and swims upright in an utterly unorthodox manner when it's not clinging to a blade of sea grass with its tail, doing its best imitation of a wisp of seaweed? Who could fail to be enthralled with a live-bearing fish in which the male gets pregnant and carries the developing young within a brood pouch like a kangaroo? What red-blooded American kid wouldn't give his two front teeth to keep such curious critters for pets?

Dwarf seahorses are very good at blending into their backgrounds. Here is a captive-bred, orange colored male.

Needless to say, the many incredible characteristics and surprising habits of these fabled fish have long made seahorses among the most desirable and highly prized of all aquarium specimens, and of all the seahorses, dwarves are perhaps the most exotic. Dwarf seahorses are a miracle of nature—endowed with all the anatomical absurdities of the greater seahorses but on a Lilliputian scale. They are mostly tail and mature at the whopping size of an inch or two. To me, their incredibly tiny size only adds to their appeal and makes them that much more of a marvel. I find them quaint and charming in the extreme. I have studied seahorses for decades and kept many species over the years, and I must confess that I'm still utterly enchanted with the idea of raising elfin creatures no bigger than my thumbnail. The diminutive dimensions of the ever-popular dwarf seahorse remain a constant delight to even an old salt like me!

They do everything their bigger brethren do, only in perfect miniature. To realize these dime-sized denizens of the deep are fully grown adults and to watch them courting, mating, and giving birth to impossibly small babies is a source of endless amazement and enjoyment.

One of the most interesting aspects about keeping dwarf seahorses is their bountiful breeding cycle. The urge to reproduce is very powerful in Hippocampus zosterae, and these pigmy ponies are prolific. They breed best when kept in groups—indeed, breeding is inevitable whenever enough dwarf seahorses are kept together under favorable conditions. The gestation period is only about ten days at standard aquarium temperatures, and gravid males normally remate within a day or two of giving birth. As a result, mature males are pregnant pretty much continuously throughout the breeding season, producing brood after brood with assembly-line regularity.

In fact, any time you purchase several pairs of dwarf seahorses at the same time during the mating season, you're virtually guaranteed to get at least a couple of pregnant males with your order as an added bonus. You can expect your first fry to be born en route in the shipping bags, shortly after they arrive, during acclimation, or immediately upon being introduced to the aquarium—or all of the above.

This is another example of a dwarf seahorse and their amazing ability to blend into their surroundings.

Best of all, they produce well-developed benthic fry and are usually considered the easiest of all seahorses to raise. The fry can be reared right alongside their parents in the same aquarium and

grow remarkably fast. They reach sexual maturity and start producing babies of their own in as little as three months, so you can expect three generations per year from these prolific ponies. More hobbyists have closed the life cycle with this species than all other seahorses put together.

Despite their small size, these dainty animals are not at all delicate. They are sturdy little fish that withstand the rigors of shipping very well and adapt easily to aquarium life. They thrive on newly hatched brine shrimp from the cradle to the grave, and the "nursery tank" for the first dwarf fry I ever raised to maturity was an ordinary mayonnaise jar I rescued from the trash.

Small wonder these miniature marvels are kept by more hobbyists than any other seahorses. Their exquisite size, toughness, ease of breeding, reasonable cost, and constant availability have made the ubiquitous dwarves by far the most widely kept species of seahorses in the U.S. from the first days of the marine aquarium hobby to the present.

Yet despite all their virtues and enormous popularity over the years, there has never been an aquarist guidebook devoted to dwarf seahorses. Such a manual is long overdue, and I can think of no better person to write such a book than Alisa Abbott, who has rapidly gained a reputation as an authority on dwarf seahorses.

By the time they reach the end of this book, the readers will realize Alisa Abbott has handed them the keys to the Kingdom of the Seahorse and unlocked the gates to a wonderland filled with breathtaking beauty, an undersea empire overflowing with unimaginable treasures and richness. It's a magical kingdom filled with spellbinding wonders and countless curiosities, and I welcome you to a lifetime of learning, beginning with your introduction to that miniature marvel of nature, the dwarf seahorse! Prepare to be enchanted.

–Pete Giwojna

Peter Giwojna is a nature writer with a strong background in biology and over 30 years of experience as a marine aquarist. He has worked with seahorses since 1987, and has published extensively on the subject of their care and husbandry in aquariums with the goal of promoting their conservation.

Introduction to Dwarf Seahorses

Dwarf Seahorses in the Wild

The dwarf seahorse has been found throughout the entire Gulf of Mexico to southern Florida and the Florida Keys, the Western Atlantic, Cuba, the Bahamas, and Bermuda. Its natural habitat is shallow grass flats, especially beds of *Zostera* and other sea grasses, as well as inshore drifting vegetation.

The inshore habitat of the dwarf seahorse means it is subject to highly variable conditions. In the bays and estuaries where they are commonly found, the influx of freshwater from torrential rains and rivers leads to changes in salinity from as much as 1.021 to 1.010 in a single day. Tides and storms bring rapidly changing water temperatures that can be every bit as extreme. The bottom is muck, rich in the rotten egg odor of hydrogen sulfide if your foot sinks in while you're wading out to the grass beds, and penetrates the oxygen-poor layers

where anaerobic decay takes place. The ability of the dwarf seahorse to thrive under such marginal conditions is a tribute to its toughness.

The reason they seek out shallow sea grass beds in such areas is the abundance of food they provide. Grass shrimp and plankton teem in the nutrient-rich grass flats.

The breeding season in the wild extends from mid-February to late October, and three generations are normally produced during that period. The breeding season is influenced by day length. Dwarf seahorses stop breeding when the period between sunrise and sunset is less than 11 hours, and reproduce best when the days are longer than 12 hours.

In some populations, females outnumber males by up to ten to one, and males are reported to fill their pouches with eggs from more than one female. This imbalanced sex ratio may contribute to the success of the dwarf seahorse as a species.

NATURAL HISTORY OF DWARF SEAHORSES

DWARF SEAHORSE CLASSIFICATION

Kingdom: Animalia (animals)

Phylum: Chordata (has a dorsal nerve cord ending at a brain)

Subphylum: Vertebrata (animals with backbones)

Subphylum: Pisces (fishes)

Class: Actinopterygii (ray-finned fishes)

Superorder: Teleostei (bony fishes)

Order: Gasterosteiformes (fishes with armored bellies)

Suborder: Syngnathoidei (fishes with fused jaws)

Family: Syngnathidae (seahorses and pipefishes)

Subfamily: Hippocampinae (seahorses)

Genus: *Hippocampus* ("horse monster")

Scientific Name: *Hippocampus zosterae* Jordan & Gilbert, 1882. The name refers to the beds of *Zostera* sea grass in which the ponies prefer to live. Other scientific names formerly used in the literature of this species, but that are now considered outdated synonyms, include *Hippocampus regulus* and *Hippocampus rosamondae*.

Common Names: Dwarf Seahorse; Pygmy or Pigmy Seahorse (U.S.); Sea Pony (U.S.)

Legend Come to Life

Taking the Reins

It's interesting to note the different reactions of people when I mention that I keep and raise seahorses. Very often, at first they appear puzzled or completely amazed, as if they're not sure I'm being serious or can't quite believe their ears. Many times their initial reaction and comments make it clear they were under the distinct impression seahorses were strictly make-believe, fictitious beasts found only in the realm of fables and fantasy. Sometimes when they get their first glimpse of real live seahorses, you hear them wonder aloud if such odd animals are actually fish at all. Others would simply comment that they have never seen a seahorse before, or that they always thought they were impossible to keep.

It's their unusual appearance and bizarre behavior that set these intriguing animals apart from any other fish in the sea and make seahorses seem slightly less than real. The facts about these

fabulous fish are far more fantastic than any fairy tale, making it difficult for some folks to take seahorses seriously. We're talking about an armored fish that has the head of a horse, a crown like a unicorn, independent eye movements like a chameleon, a prehensile tail like a monkey to hold on to things, and, get this—the male gives birth and has a pouch like a kangaroo!

Given the seahorse's many unfishlike features, it's hard to blame people for being skeptical when you explain to them that these unorthodox animals are true fish, complete with fins, gills, and a swim bladder. But that's part of what makes keeping seahorses so much fun!

How I Got Started

For many years, I was among the many people who thought that these amazing animals were forever beyond my reach, to be experienced only through photographs, books, and nature documentaries. Sure, I knew of their existence and always wanted them as a child, but trying to convince Mom and Dad to get some was impossible. Like myself, my parents and so many others were under the impression that people just did not keep seahorses. Why, they are such exotic, delicate creatures that it would be like putting a butterfly on a leash, caging a hummingbird, or keeping a pet mermaid!

In spite of it all, I always insisted that when I grew up, I was going to keep seahorses. If you are a parent, you can imagine what my folks thought of that. No doubt they considered my early aspirations to be no more than childish, wishful thinking, as if I had blithely announced my intention to become an astronaut, a ballerina, or a movie star. Well, I am now a grown-up–or like to believe I am—and sure enough, I do indeed have seahorses. Lots of 'em, all kinds and ages, courting like crazy, breeding, having babies, thriving, just like I said I would. (Look, Mom and Dad—seahorses!)

But getting there wasn't easy. When I first started with seahorses, I made plenty of painful mistakes and learned from them, the hard way.

The first time I ever saw a real live seahorse was when I opened up a little shipping box I received in the mail from an order I made online. I quickly, but oh so carefully, opened the little box and held my breath, praying that they were alive. I am not sure what I expected to see, but there in a little bag was a pair of tiny seahorses. They really did look like all the pictures in the books I had seen! I was so excited, it was love at first sight.

About two weeks before that fateful day, I had stumbled across a website advertising the sale of dwarf seahorses while doing some research on the Internet. I was delighted to read that they were as easy to keep as guppies, and since the site included instructions on how to feed them, I took the plunge and ordered the complete kit: brine shrimp cysts, a little packet of sea salt, a tiny betta bowl to serve as their new home, a plastic plant, and a pair of seahorses. Why not, I reasoned—they're easy to keep and I have kept guppies before with no problems.

Here is a good example of a pale yellow and white male dwarf seahorse.

Mother's Little Helpers: peering intently at two of her offspring, which may total 50 or more fry in all, this striped female appears to have her hands full.

If you know anything about fish keeping or saltwater aquarium requirements—and most likely you do since you are obviously reading this because of an interest in getting some of your very own seahorses—then you are probably cringing at the very thought of how I was going about keeping these beautiful fish. Heaven knows I am wincing even as I write this! I am sure that by now you have already figured out that I did not have my first seahorses very long. Back then I didn't even know enough to cringe at my lack of knowledge. All I knew was that my first seahorses had finally arrived and they were exactly as I had always imagined. All was right with the world…for a few days anyway.

Keeping Dwarf Seahorses

An astonishing array of unique characteristics, combined with the ability to change color, pretty much sums up the seahorse, an exotic marine tropical that to this day remains as mysterious to most as the mermaid of myth. The Dwarf Seahorse (*Hippocampus zosterae*) is one of the smallest species of all. As adults they reach 1 to 1.5 inches in length, and that includes the length of their tail.

Dwarf seahorses are typically brown or white but can sometimes be yellow, yellow with black bands, white with polka dots, black, and even green. During courtship and mating the seahorse will change colors, trying to impress their mate. I have seen them turn from brown to almost pink, and to various shades of yellow, green, white, or cream. These transformations can be quite captivating since seahorses use color for camouflage and communication as well as courtship. Awe-inspiring color changes reflect the seahorse's mood, environment, and readiness to breed.

Dwarf seahorses are a surprisingly hardy fish and adapt well to the home aquarium. They are one of the few species of seahorses that can live on a staple diet of

Dwarf seahorses are very good at blending into their backgrounds. Here is a captive-bred, orange colored male.

live, newly hatched brine shrimp, which you can easily hatch at home. They breed readily in the home aquarium, and each male will give birth to anywhere between 3 and 35 fry, with an average brood size of about 18 in captivity.

This brings us to another interesting fact about seahorses that we touched upon earlier: it is the male that gets pregnant and delivers the young! The female will deposit her eggs into the pouch of the male, where he will fertilize and support them until

birth. Gestation is about 10 to 14 days. Dwarves are by far the most social of the seahorses. They interact well with each other and perform a wonderful mating ritual that will totally amaze anyone, which we will discuss in the section on breeding.

Dwarf seahorses generally live for about one year in the wild but can be kept for two to three years or more in the home aquarium if proper care is provided. In order to give them a better life than they could hope for in the ocean, however, the seahorse keeper must be prepared to pick up some special equipment.

Setting Up the Aquarium 2

Aquarium Selection

Once you've decided that you would like to keep dwarf seahorses, it is very important to consider their new home and what best suits you as the hobbyist. I generally recommend a 5-gallon setup; this will happily house quite a number of dwarves. The minimum number of dwarves I would keep in a 5-gallon tank is five pairs.

The reason for this is food concentration. You will probably be feeding them live brine shrimp that you hatch at home, and achieving the proper feeding density is one of the keys to keeping dwarf seahorses. Brine shrimp are very small, and to ensure seahorses receive plenty of food without having so much that all the excess shrimp die off, you want to house enough dwarves to compensate for the amount of brine shrimp you are adding. Seahorses can be very lazy and typically wait for food to come to them. Dwarf seahorses can starve themselves if enough brine does not pass right under their little snouts.

THE TANK

If you feel more comfortable with a smaller setup, a 2-gallon tank can be used as well, but always keep in mind that the smaller the tank, the more quickly water quality can deteriorate. I personally have kept dwarves in tanks ranging from 1 gallon to 10 gallons. In a 10-gallon you would want a minimum of one dozen dwarves. Anything much larger than a 10-gallon aquarium is not recommended for dwarves.

If you have experience with keeping saltwater fishes and want to buy a larger herd of seahorses, then go ahead and start off with the 10-gallon. If you are new to the hobby, you should get either a 2-gallon or a 5-gallon tank and start out with fewer seahorses. Remember, you can always upgrade later on as your population and experience increase.

The dimensions and shape of the tank are not that important with dwarves. For the larger species of seahorses, optimum tank height should be three times the length of your seahorse, so if you have 6-inch seahorses you would need a water column at

Here a common, or wild-type, male is holding onto a piece of Halimeda.

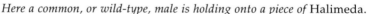

least 18 inches tall. Tank height is more important than width or length when it comes to seahorses, but since dwarves only reach about 1.5 inches in length, you do not need to concern yourself so much with height of the tank.

Glass and acrylic are both acceptable, but remember that acrylic scratches easily. There is no need to run out and buy one of those nifty setups with all the special equipment and filters, because most of that will not be needed and they can be costly. With dwarf seahorses, a simple setup is most economical and most reliable.

LIGHTING

As for the lighting, you can use your own preference. I have 15-watt bulbs in my 10-gallon tanks and that is plenty for my macroalgae, zoanthids, and sponges. Intense lighting is not recommended because seahorses can be so lazy and slow that algae often grow on their bodies. Such algal growth is generally not harmful, but I find it to be unsightly.

Regardless of the size of your seahorse ranch, it is important to monitor water quality closely. I do monthly water changes in my 10-gallon tank and add fresh water weekly. In a smaller tank you will probably be required to do more frequent water changes. Do not let this alarm you as this is not difficult to do and is not costly for small setups like these.

Another consideration to keep in mind while selecting a tank is where you plan on keeping it. Do not keep your tank near a window, air-conditioner, or heat source because temperatures may fluctuate too much in small setups and cause stress in your seahorses, which may result in illness.

Choosing A Substrate

I have found over the years that choosing the substrate is one of the most important considerations when setting up a tank for dwarf seahorses. Hobbyists often ask me which substrate is best to use or express concern because they have heard rumors that a particular type of substrate is undesirable for seahorses. I have tried many kinds.

BLACK SAND

At present, my preference happens to be black sand. One reason I favor it is because black sand seems to show off the coloration variations of the seahorses better, makes them more visible, and shows off marine plants and aquarium décor exceptionally well. I also can view their fry better and it is a lot easier to find any fry that may have died. It looks cleaner to me, and I can spot unwanted critters that may have decided to make themselves at home in the tank such as hydroids, dangerous pests that I will discuss in more depth later.

On the move, this male dwarf seahorse reveals its beautifully banded tail.

I have had no trouble maintaining good water quality, and so far my pH has never appeared to be affected by using black sand. I have been using black sand exclusively for the past two years and am highly pleased with it, as are many others who have tried it. However, the use of black sand still generates a lot of controversy, and no doubt you will come across many different opinions about using it if that is your choice.

In general, other types of saltwater-safe sand, such as silica and aragonite, are also good choices. However, using a live sand bed should be avoided if you are a newcomer as it may contain some unwanted critters that may not be dwarf-friendly, such as hydroids, certain dangerous shrimp (mantis shrimp and pistol shrimp), and large bristle worms. Small bristle worms are actually fine and make a good clean up crew, but they are not needed to maintain a successful tank.

I have heard many rumors that sand, in general, can be harmful to seahorses because they may accidentally suck up sand when feeding on bottom-hugging prey, but in my experience such concerns are totally unfounded. As denizens of sea grass beds in shallow water, sand is certainly part of the dwarf seahorse's natural environment. Will they occasionally snick it up? Sure. I have seen this with the larger seahorse species especially, and they always simply spit or blow it out again. I have never had a seahorse come to harm snicking up sand. I have, though, seen one of my larger seahorses suck up a piece of crushed coral and suffer temporary distress from this, but with no lasting harmful effects.

CRUSHED CORAL

Other popular choices for substrate include crushed coral and/or crushed shell. I have used both of these as well and found them to be satisfactory. However, crushed coral is quite coarse and scratchy and does not offer as much surface area for potential biological filtration as does sand, but I did not observe any particular problems when I used it.

Pregnant Papa: a male dwarf seahorse nearing the end of its 10-14 day gestation period.

BARE BOTTOM

If sand, crushed coral, and shell are not enough options, there is always the bare-bottom setup. This is one method I personally do not care for unless you are setting up a separate nursery tank. The reasons I do not favor a bare-bottom are because it provides no supplemental biological filtration, more water changes may be required as a result, and the bottom gets dirty fast, giving the appearance of an unkempt tank.

The primary benefit of a bare bottom setup is cleanliness. A bare bottom facilitates water changes and aquarium

maintenance. It makes it easy to spot leftovers, remove uneaten food, and siphon off the bottom, preventing the accumulation of detritus. But the trade-off is that such maintenance must be performed on a daily basis or the tank looks unsightly, and the sterile look of the barren bottom is unnatural and unattractive. It's a good option for nursery tanks where cleanliness is paramount and daily water changes are mandatory, but it is not recommended for a display tank.

Other substrates that are available include your typical aquarium gravel and natural rock. I generally avoid them because I prefer the more natural look and other benefits a sand substrate provides.

The Aquarium Background

The aquarium background is one of those things that you either forget about or have been obsessed with since you first decided you wanted a seahorse corral. In a seahorse tank, not

This photo shows a pale colored male hitched to an orange gorgonian.

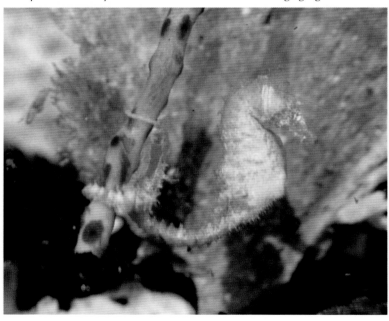

only does a background add to the aquarium's aesthetic beauty but also contributes often to the coloration of the seahorses as well. In their natural environment, seahorses blend into their surrounding as a natural means of defense. True masters of camouflage, dwarf seahorses will do the same in your tank.

Given their chameleon-like color changes, selecting a bright aquarium backing will often encourage seahorses to display bright colors. Interestingly, the results are not always what you would expect.

For instance, when I added a fluorescent pink background, my dwarves changed to different variations of yellow, much to my surprise. I have noticed that either a pink or a bright orange backing tends to elicit the most dramatic color changes in my seahorses, including the larger species. Yet, for some reason, a red background does not have that much of an effect.

White backgrounds, and even a white substrate, often have the opposite effect, causing the seahorse's color to fade, which is another reason I favor a black substrate. Mildred Bellomy, author of *Encyclopedia of Sea Horses*, describes a perfect example of this:

This is another example of a dwarf seahorse and their amazing ability to blend into their surroundings.

"One time, I brought in a dwarf sea horse and installed it in a two-and-one-half gallon aquarium sitting on top of a triangular insert which formed part of the seat in my breakfast nook. One of the decorative hitching posts placed in the aquarium was a piece of pure-white, finger coral.

"On the afternoon of collection and placement in the tank, the small male horse was fawn-colored with lighter, almost white, mottling. When I got up the next morning, I looked to see how my small pet was faring. I could not find him. I looked and looked and looked, and finally convinced myself he was not in the tank. This simply could not be. A sea horse just doesn't vanish! Moreover, it wasn't possible for that small specimen to flip out of a tank that was only three-quarters full of water, nor could my pet have provided a meal for another fish. There was no other living thing in the aquarium except some tiny freshly hatched brine shrimp. I ran for my hand lens, and began an inch-by-inch, through-the-front-glass search of everything in the tank.

"I was so relieved I wasn't even slightly provoked when I found my pet had deceived what, up to that time, I had considered a pair of eyes trained to locate camouflaged sea animals. There he was— wearing a coat that exactly matched the whiteness of the piece of finger coral atop which he perched so serenely immovable that he might have been a part of it." (1969, Encyclopedia of Sea Horses, T.F.H. Publications, Inc., p. 32)

Here is a captive-bred, orange colored male.

Although factors such as black sand, colorful décor, and a bright aquarium background can all contribute to enhancing their color, I am afraid that dwarves are simply not considered to be among the most colorful of seahorses. They are adapted to blend into a sea grass habitat and are adept at mimicking the seasonal color changes of the vast *Zostera* beds that they are named after. Their pigmentation thus tends toward the earth tones: everything from black, brown, and beige to assorted grays and off-whites to various shades of yellow and olive or mint green. Vivid hues like red, violet, blue, and chartreuse just don't seem to be in their repertoire. Most specimens are a mottled brown, fawn, or a dirty white, but by employing unique color schemes like those described above, the hobbyist can bring out the brightest shades in his seahorses, show them off to their best effects, and assure that his or her dwarves will stand out and be more noticeable.

Decorations and Hitching Posts

As ambush predators, seahorses spend most of their time hitched in place, patiently waiting for prey to pass within easy reach. Whether the seahorses are simply resting or hunting, they need plenty of convenient places to hitch onto. Seahorse trees are a favorite for this. They do not alter the chemistry of your tank and look very attractive and natural. Seahorse trees can be bought at some local fish stores or purchased online. They are inexpensive and can accommodate many seahorses. They sort of remind me of a sparse Charlie Brown Christmas tree, only decorated with the most exquisite, animated ornaments imaginable—living seahorses.

Dwarf seahorses breed best when kept in groups, as shown here. They are polygamous ponies and reproductive success improves when they can choose from a number of prospective partners.

Here we see several dwarf seahorses linked together tail-to-snout-to-torso-to-tail to form a living chain of ponies. Dwarf seahorses are highly gregarious animals that are accustomed to living in densely populated colonies.

Another favorite hitching post for dwarves is *Caulerpa* macroalgae; not only do seahorses love this but it is also healthy for your tank. It will provide a welcome touch of greenery and help to hold nitrate levels down by consuming them for growth. Trimming and harvesting your lush growth of *Caulerpa* regularly will actually remove nitrate from your tank. *Caulerpa* grows very well in the aquarium, and there are many different types to choose from.

Filtration Options

There are many different types of filtration units available for the hobbyist to choose from, but due to the small size of dwarf seahorses, most of these units are not recommended. The intakes of most filters are too powerful and will easily suck up an adult dwarf. I have seen this happen in my tank before and hear about this happening to others all of the time. However, this does not mean there are not ways around this problem. You can always modify one of these filters by placing a sponge over the intake or use filter floss inside to decrease the suction.

SPONGE FILTERS

My suggestion is just to use an ordinary air-operated sponge filter. They are very cost-effective and reliable, and I have never had a problem with water quality when using them with dwarf seahorses. There are many different brands of sponge or foam filters, and most are acceptable. An exception was one type that contained a metal disc that unfortunately bled rust into one of my tanks. When used in salt water, always avoid sponge filters with any metal components. When used in conjunction with sand, I find a simple sponge filter provides excellent mechanical and biological filtration.

Foam or sponge filters are simple, economical, foolproof, and very versatile. It's a good idea to keep a couple of extra sponge filters on hand at all times, preferably precycled in a sump or an out-of-the way nook in another well-established marine tank. That way, they can serve as portable, instant biofilters whenever and wherever they're needed—for an extra nursery or hospital tank, a new setup, as supplemental filtration for your main tank as your herd increases, or anywhere biofiltration has been compromised.

This photo shows a nice green and yellow male dwarf seahorse. Notice the white striping on the tail.

Cleaning them is quite easy. Simply immerse the sponge filter in a bucket of saltwater and gently squeeze it out until no more debris is released. Wipe the plastic tubing clean inside and out and you're done. It takes only a few minutes and the sponge filter is back in action with no impairment of its biological filtration ability.

The Risks of Live Rock

Live rock filtration in conjunction with mechanical filtration is valued by many marine hobbyists including myself, and I always use live rock for my larger seahorse species. However, just like the live sand, live rock can house some unwanted critters that are dangerous to dwarf seahorses. Rock anemones (*Aiptasia*) and hydroids are the biggest and ugliest threats in that regard. Although you will probably not see any hydroids on the live rock you intend to use, once you add the rock to the tank they often appear as if by magic. The constant supply of baby brine shrimp hobbyists provide for dwarf seahorses creates the perfect environment to help *Aiptasia* and hydroids colonize and grow, and these stinging animals can kill your dwarf fry. Even some adult dwarves can succumb to multiple stings or to secondary infections following a bad sting. It's best to avoid live rock in small dwarf seahorse setups for this reason.

This does not mean rock cannot be used at all. You can place dry or "dead" rock in your tank and in no time at all it will become overgrown with lush algae and populated with a multitude of organisms, and you will have created your own live rock safely. The beneficial bacteria needed for biological filtration will quickly grow on and within the porous rock.

Proper Care and Maintenance

of the Aquarium

What You Should Know

Although captive raised seahorses are considerably hardier than their wild cousins, they must still be given the proper aquarium conditions in order to thrive in aquaria. Hobbyists need to understand the importance of water chemistry and how it relates to their success with seahorses. Some areas of water chemistry are more crucial to focus your understanding on than others. For example, salinity and the nitrogen cycle are by far the most important characteristics the average hobbyist will need to understand.

Salinity

The specific gravity or salinity level of the salt water is important. You use a hydrometer to check the specific gravity. A more accurate reading can be taken with a refractometer, but most people rely on a hydrometer. They are fairly reliable,

This male dwarf seahorse is hitched to a gorgonian skeleton. Notice the pipefish in the background.

inexpensive, and if kept clean should last a couple of years. The most commonly used and most convenient are the plastic types in which you collect some water from your tank and place it in the tester. The water raises a movable, plastic arm to point out the results on a scale.

There is also the cylindrical glass type that often has a built-in thermometer as well. To use this kind of hydrometer and get the most accurate results, you will need to collect water from your tank and place it in a separate clean container, making sure to fill it with enough water so that the bottom of the floating hydrometer does not touch the bottom of the cylinder. The whole hydrometer will bob up and down, so get the reading after it settles down and the water stabilizes and becomes calm; take the reading where the meniscus or waterline touches the scale on the stem of the hydrometer.

Dwarf seahorses do best at readings ranging from 1.019 to 1.021, but for some reason I have found that they seem to be most active and court more often when the specific gravity is maintained at 1.019. To help keep your specific gravity at a constant level, you can mark the waterline on the tank when the hydrometer reading is at the 1.019 mark. As the water evaporates, you can simply add more conditioned fresh water to reach the line you marked on the tank. Remember that only the water evaporates, leaving the salt behind, so just top off your tank with fresh water—there is usually no need to add more salt.

SALT CREEP

You will at some point start noticing an accumulation of dried salt around the rim of the aquarium. These deposits are the result of salt spray and capillary action and are know as salt creep. The deposits are harmless but unsightly, giving the top of your tank an ugly, crusty appearance. They can easily be removed by rinsing the top of the aquarium with water.

A helpful hint when doing water changes: I recommend that you premix and aerate the salt water at least 24 hours prior to the water change. This will help ensure oxygenation and make sure that the salt mix dissolves completely. Newly mixed salt water can contain low levels of ammonia, and waiting the 24 hours will remove these trace levels.

Understanding the Nitrogen Cycle

The nitrogen cycle is the key to establishing your biofilter and ultimately the key to building a foundation for your dwarf seahorse aquarium. Unfortunately, you just cannot go out and buy a tank, set it up, and add seahorses. You must first cycle your tank. This is the natural process where your tank will undergo a series of changes to build up its own natural

This small green colored dwarf is perched on a small piece of live rock.

biological filter, composed of beneficial bacteria that convert nitrogenous waste products to relatively harmless byproducts. This process is known as the nitrogen cycle. It generally takes about three to six weeks to complete the nitrogen cycle when first setting up an aquarium.

AMMONIA TO NITRATE

The nitrogen cycle begins with ammonia, a highly toxic substance that is deadly to all fishes. Ammonia enters an aquarium in a number of ways. The decay of plant matter, uneaten fish food, and other organic substances produce ammonia. Like all animals, seahorses also produce ammonia though their normal metabolic processes such as breathing, eliminating, and excreting urine.

As your tank cycles, a population of beneficial *Nitrosomonas* bacteria will build up and convert the ammonia to nitrite. This is the first step in the nitrogen cycle. The nitrite produced by these *Nitrosomonas* bacteria is also very toxic to fish. During the second step in the nitrogen cycle, beneficial *Nitrobacter* bacteria begin to build up and convert the nitrite to relatively harmless nitrate. Nitrate is not dangerous unless it builds up to excessive levels.

Under anaerobic—oxygen poor— conditions, such as that beneath a properly constructed, deep, sand bed or within the interior of live rock, denitrifying bacteria will then begin to grow and break down the nitrate to nitrogen. The nitrogen this produces leaves the tank through bubbles of nitrogen gas, thus completing the nitrogen cycle. Through the nitrogen cycle, the toxic ammonia we began with was first converted to poisonous nitrite, then converted to nontoxic nitrate, and finally converted to harmless nitrogen gas and exported from the tank.

This final step in the cycle, the conversion of nitrate to nitrogen, does *not* occur in typical dwarf seahorse setups due to the exclusion of live rock and deep live sand beds in the interests of pest control. Dwarf seahorse keepers must therefore take other

Here is a pale lime green male dwarf seahorse.

steps to prevent nitrate from building up to harmful levels. This is usually accomplished through regular water changes.

WHY YOU MUST CYCLE YOUR AQUARIUM

When cycling your tank and establishing your biofilter, it takes time for the population of beneficial bacteria to build up sufficiently to handle the nitrogenous waste products at each step in your process. That is why it takes from three to six weeks to complete the entire cycling process and why you cannot add seahorses to an aquarium that does not have a fully functional

biofilter. If you do, their wastes will build up unchecked until the seahorses die from ammonia poisoning. Your tank must therefore be cycled to establish the biological filtration *before* you get your seahorses.

There are a number of ways to accomplish this. Two popular methods are the fishless cycle, which I recommend, and the use of hardy, inexpensive (i.e., expendable) fish to produce ammonia and cycle the aquarium. Often used for this method are marine damselfish or mollies, which can be easily converted to salt water. Both are very hardy and generally survive the cycling process, but I find this method to be needlessly hard on the fish, and exposing them to the toxic ammonia and nitrite produced during cycling certainly causes them stress. This can be avoided altogether by cycling the tank without fish.

> ### WATER QUALITY GUIDELINES
> *Establish your dwarf seahorse ranch to conform to the following parameters and strive for stability within the suggested readings:*
> - *Temperature: 70 degrees F - 80 degrees F (21 degrees C – 27 degrees C), optimum 75 degrees F*
> - *Specific gravity: 1.018 to 1.022, optimum 1.019*
> - *pH: 8.2-8.4*
> - *Ammonia: 0*
> - *Nitrite: 0*
> - *Nitrate: 0-10ppm.*

To use the fishless cycle, we need to add something else that will increase the ammonia level so the nitrifying bacteria can build up. I like to use either frozen mysid shrimp or a piece of cocktail shrimp. I leave this in the tank to decay during the whole cycle. After about three days you will notice a spike in ammonia levels until the *Nitrosomonas* bacteria build up enough to break down the ammonia. When that happens, you will notice the ammonia levels rapidly dropping. If for some reason your ammonia did not hit the top of the charts, you may want to add another piece of shrimp. The byproduct of ammonia is nitrite, and during this stage of the cycling process you will have an increase in nitrites until the population of *Nitrobacter* bacteria builds up. Nitrite levels will then fall as the *Nitrobacter* convert the nitrite to nitrate.

It is important to use your test kits every day or two when cycling your tank to monitor the progress of the process. As described above, at first you will see a rapid rise in ammonia levels with no detectable nitrite or nitrate. Then, as *Nitrosomonas* bacteria begin converting ammonia to nitrite, the ammonia levels will fall and nitrite readings will steadily rise. Nitrite levels will peak as the ammonia drops to zero. Next, *Nitrobacter* will begin converting the nitrite to nitrate, and your nitrite readings will fall as the level of nitrate rises. Finally, after the nitrites also read zero, you are ready to stock your tank. At this point, your ammonia and nitrite levels should both be zero. This will tell you that your biofilter is active and functioning properly, and that you can now safely add your seahorses. The byproduct of the breakdown of nitrite is nitrate, of course, and you will be doing regular water changes from now on to control nitrate levels.

Here is a black beauty perched on feathery frond of Caulerpa.

Using Macroalgae
CAULERPA SPP.

Another method of reducing nitrate levels in the dwarf seahorse tank is through growing and regularly harvesting the bright green seaweed (an alga) *Caulerpa*, which utilizes nitrate for growth. *Caulerpa* absorbs great amounts of nitrates and converts them in its cells. By periodically removing reasonable quantities of the seaweed from the tank, nitrates also are removed from the cycle. Growing *Caulerpa* helps keep the tank cleaner and also beautifies it and provides some hitches for your seahorses.

HALIMEDA SPP.

This group of macroalgae is well known to those who scuba dive off the coast of Florida and throughout the tropical Atlantic and Caribbean oceans. *Halimeda* is a type of calcareous algae and performs the duties of shrubbery and herbs on the seafloor. When a plant dies off, its skeleton will decompose and form a small amount of sand. Over many years, and many die-offs, *Halimeda* can contribute significantly to the reef-building process.

Seahorses that inhabit coral reefs and deeper waters use various species of *Halimeda* as hitching posts. In the aquarium, *Halimeda* is often difficult to maintain. It needs strong lighting and excellent water quality, but when you get a good batch going, it is often very beautiful and worth the effort.

PENICILLUS CAPITATUS

Often called Neptune's shaving brush, or simply, shaving brush plant, *P. capitatus* is a very common calcareous-algae in the shallower depths of the tropical Atlantic. It is easily recognized by its long stalk and tuft of bristle-like branches at the top. Healthy specimens are a bright green color with a thick stalk that can grow as tall as six inches.

Seahorses wrap their prehensile tails around the stalk in order to be covered by the bush at the top of the vegetation. *H. zosterae* can often be found among the green branches due to their size. Shaving brush needs a very strong light and a mild current in order to thrive in captivity. It is recommended that you only put this species of algae in setups that have been designed for it.

Stocking Your Ranch

4

Selecting Healthy Animals

After deciding what size aquarium best suits your needs, your next decision will be where to purchase your specimen, either from an online vendor or a fish store. There are several online vendors to choose from, which will enable you to purchase dwarf seahorses directly from the collector and deliver them straight to your doorstep. Until very recently, unless you knew someone who raised them, the only readily available dwarf seahorses were wild-caught specimens from Florida. From time to time I offered some of my tank-raised dwarves to fellow hobbyists, and there were other successful breeders out there who would do the same, but the vast majority of dwarf seahorse keepers had to settle for wild specimens.

However, this now has changed. Several companies are becoming famous for their farm-raised dwarf seahorses. The captive raised stock is more expensive than wild *Hippocampus zosterae*

This pregnant male has taken up residency on a nice piece of **Caulerpa**.

but are eco-friendly and parasite-free, giving the dwarf seahorse keeper more options than ever. The odds are good that more commercial breeders will begin offering dwarves for sale and that these seahorses will become readily available almost everywhere.

Most fish stores do not handle dwarf seahorses because of the difficulty and expense of providing them with live brine shrimp on a daily basis. If you are lucky enough to find a local fish shop that carries dwarves, be sure to ask them how long they have had them, what they are fed, and how often. If it turns out they do not feed their dwarf seahorses regularly or offer them inappropriate foods (basically anything other than newly hatched brine shrimp), look elsewhere for dwarf seahorses that are not malnourished and half-starved.

WHAT TO LOOK FOR

Should you find well-fed dwarves that are eating well at your local shop, there are several other things to look at before

purchasing them; this applies to any type of seahorse. First you will want to observe the general appearance of the seahorse. When observed head-on, their belly should be rounded slightly or straight in cross-section, *not* sunken in or concave. Watch their eye movements closely. Seahorses have eyes that work independently on either side of their heads, and they are constantly scanning their surroundings. A healthy seahorse should display active eye movements.

Normal coloration is also a very important sign of health. Although dwarf seahorses have a wide variety of colorations and patterns, watch out for abnormal gray or white blotches or patches, particularly if they are not repeated on both sides of the body. If you observe any suspicious patches or splotches, do not purchase those specimens because they may be afflicted by a bacterial or fungal infection. Look closely at their snouts, and check for any redness or abnormalities. Make a point of watching the seahorses eat, and if you see any having difficulty snicking up food, it's a surefire indication of an unhealthy seahorse.

Here several color variants of dwarf seahorses are together on a single hitching post. This photo allows you to see the amazing diversity in coloration between specimens.

How Many is Too Many?

I am sure your next question is "How many should I get?" I hear this question often and, of course, the proper stocking level depends on the size of your corral. Let's start off by considering a 2-gallon tank, which is the smallest aquarium I would recommend as a permanent home for dwarf seahorses. For a 2-gallon tank, a nice figure to start off with is two or three pairs. You may certainly get more, but remember these guys are

A close-up of several dwarf seahorses with babies.

fast breeders, and with any luck at all you will soon have 30 or 40 of them with more on the way. I do not recommend keeping more than eight adults and perhaps 60 fry in a 2-gallon tank, a stocking density that will require frequent water changes and diligent maintenance in order to maintain good water quality.

You will most likely lose most of the fry by their second week, at least during your first few attempts to rear the babies. I know this is a frightening thought, but I assure you that this is a normal part of the learning curve and happens with most hobbyists. As you gain more experience and work out your own special rearing method, you will find that you lose fewer fry with each batch of young. With these prolific little seahorses, you will have plenty of opportunities to hone your skills and learn from your initial mistakes.

Each breeding pair will produce a new brood approximately every two weeks, and with six to eight adults chances are that you will have more than one pregnant male at any given time.

Before you know it, you will be raising some of the babies from each brood to maturity. This is a great accomplishment and a very satisfying achievement, since you are now offering the fry a better chance of survival than they would have out in the wild—in the wild, only less than one in a thousand will survive to maturity. These enchanting animals grow remarkably fast, reaching sexual maturity within three to four months, so even if you are starting with just two to four pairs of adults, your herd will increase rapidly.

If you have a 5-gallon tank set up for your dwarf seahorses, it's best to start out with no fewer then eight to ten adults. A few extra pairs of hungry seahorses help to offset the greater amount of brine shrimp you will be adding to maintain an adequate feeding density in a tank of this size. In a 5-gallon tank, you will have the freedom to allow your seahorse population to grow much larger than a 2-gallon aquarium can accommodate. I am not going to try and average out the best ratio of adults to fry to maintain in a 5-gallon setup because there are just too many variables to consider, but in one of my 5-gallons I had about 20 adults and over 50 fry at one point, and my water quality was not adversely affected. I did do weekly water changes, though, since fry can really foul up a tank fast due to their heavy feeding requirements.

For those of you who want to go all out and use a 10-gallon tank, I would get no less than six pairs or 12 adults for the reasons stated above. Both the 5-gallon and 10-gallon tanks are great for dwarves and allow greater numbers of dwarf seahorses and their fry to be kept, as well as providing a more stable environment for yourself and your specimens due to the increased volume of water. This is another consideration to keep in mind, but it should not be the main factor when choosing your tank because you can successfully keep dwarves in any of the sizes I have mentioned. Remember, the bigger the tank, the more brine shrimp that will be needed to feed your dwarves and the more difficult it becomes to maintain a sufficient feeding density, especially when rearing fry.

Acclimating Your Seahorses

At long last the big moment has arrived and the time has come to stock your tank. After those seemingly endless weeks of waiting while your tank cycled, your patience is about to be rewarded and you are finally ready to add seahorses to your corral.

Dwarf seahorses generally tolerate shipping well and acclimate with surprising quickness. They will usually eat right away, looking as though they haven't a care in the world. Some may try to court shortly after being introduced into their new establishment. If you have a pregnant male, this is often when they give birth, so you will want to have some food on hand ready for them to graze on.

The brine shrimp hatching process generally takes 24 to 36 hours, which is why I suggest hatching them two days ahead of time. It's comforting to know your seahorses will have food right away, and anything you can do to reduce stress on yourself and your new arrivals is well worth doing. We often forget such details at the last moment because we are concerned with so many other things, and the sheer excitement alone can make us forget about the "little" things like this.

Arrival

I am assuming you have mail-ordered your seahorses, but these instructions apply equally well if you're bringing your dwarves home from a local fish store. The first thing you must do is open the box away from bright lights. (Avoid taking your seahorses from total darkness into bright light—with no eyelids to close, this can be stressful to fish.)

This is when we generally hold our breaths, not knowing what to expect, wondering if the bag had a leak and released all of the water, or if the trip was too hard on them. Yes, this is an anxious moment—the time we all entertain our worst fears and dreads. No one wants to open the box to see a dead seahorse. To this day, I still feel that same sense of breathless suspense and anticipation whenever I get a new shipment. Although it is very rare, I have in the past received a seahorse that was dead

Here is a captive produced male of the "orange" variety.

when it arrived. Reputable companies guarantee live delivery and will offer you a replacement if deaths occur, but this is very infrequent with dwarf seahorses.

Once you have pulled the bag out of the shipping box, pour the water and seahorses into a separate clean container. Floating the shipping bag in your aquarium is not recommended. The outside of the bag is dirty and the water quality in the bag is poor and only gets worse once the bag is opened and fresh oxygen hits the water. For this reason, I suggest that acclimating should always be done in a separate container. You can use a bowl or Mason jar for this; just about any clean, inert container free of soaps and chemicals will do nicely.

PREVENTING SHOCK!

Acclimating your seahorses is a very crucial step. This will prevent shock from any sudden changes in the pH, temperature, and specific gravity (SG). Here are some items that will make the acclimation process a lot easier: small acclimation container, turkey baster, container of fresh water, and a temporary holding tank. Formalin that you can add to the fresh water is optional.

Carefully pour the contents of the bag into the container, watching to make sure no seahorses stick to the bag and get stranded out of the water. If they do, wet your fingers and gently pick them up and place them into their acclimating container. Draw up some water from their new home and slowly add it to their container (one of the many aquarium uses for the versatile turkey baster). I generally acclimate my seahorses over a period of 30 to 45 minutes, slowly releasing a turkey baster full of water every few minutes until the acclimating container holds approximately equal amounts of new water added from the aquarium and the shipping water they came in.

Another light colored, captive produced male dwarf seahorse.

Once a 50/50 mixture of new tank water and old shipping water has been achieved, draw out some of the water from the acclimating container and discard it so more aquarium water can be added. I generally remove about a third or more of the water and then continue adding more water from their new home until about 75 percent or more of the container consists of water from their new home.

Freshwater Dip

The next step is the freshwater dip. I am certain this sounds a little scary and more than a little intimidating, and it was for me the first few times as well. Rest assured that this step is crucial for removing parasites that may be attached to your dwarf seahorses and that it is also very safe. Ectoparasites are a common problem with wild seahorses, and the risk of introducing them to your aquarium can be safely and easily prevented with a simple, brief, freshwater dip. You can use aged tap water, spring water, or RO/DI (Reverse Osmosis/Deionized) water for the dip, but I do not recommend distilled water for dips or baths.

Although pH is very important and a sudden change can be hazardous to saltwater fish, I have found that equalizing the pH is not necessary for the short duration of the freshwater dip.

The temperature, however, is another matter. The temperature of the fresh water used for the dip *must* be the same as the temperature of the salt water the seahorses are in to avoid thermal shock. The temperatures can be equalized simply by putting some fresh water (which will be used for the dips) into a clean bag and floating that for a while in the holding or quarantine tank the seahorses will be transferred to following the dip.

Handling fish with your hands should always be kept to a minimum, but there are times when handling seahorses by hand is necessary and the safest option. Dipping them is one such time, since we never want to net dwarf seahorses because their tiny fins and sensitive snouts can easily become tangled in the netting and damaged. Wet

There are so many different colors to choose from with dwarf seahorses! Here is a fine example of a green color phase.

your hands first so you won't remove too much of the seahorses' protective slime coating when you handle them, and then ever-so-gently grasp one of the dwarves and place it into the freshwater bath, timing the dip for two to four minutes.

Observe the seahorse closely during the dip, and if you see it lying down before time has elapsed, don't hesitate to remove it early and transfer the seahorse to the holding tank. As long

as the seahorse is behaving normally and showing no signs of distress, keep it in the fresh water for the full four minutes. Repeat the dipping procedure with each seahorse one at a time. Although it sounds very intimidating, I have never lost a seahorse during a freshwater dip, and I cannot emphasize enough the importance of dipping seahorses.

From Holding Tank to Home

The holding tank itself can be very simple. You can use any clear, inert container with a capacity of at least 1 to 2 gallons. Fill it with salt water taken from the newly cycled aquarium you have set up to be their permanent home. No substrate or filter is needed.

You can use an airline for aeration, but this usually is not crucial unless you notice your seahorses gasping for air, something I have never seen happen during the brief quarantine period. They will remain isolated in this tank for only three days, purging any hydroids the dwarf seahorses may be carrying.

This male dwarf has just been placed in his new home. It may take several hours for your new seahorses to adjust and feel comfortable.

THEIR PERMANENT HOME

After three days of isolation in the holding tank, it's time for the big move to their permanent quarters. This is yet another exciting time, since you will finally be able to watch your seahorses interact and go about their everyday activities in the perfect and loving environment you so carefully created for them. Congratulations!

But before you eagerly transfer them in their new home, you need to give them all one last freshwater bath. This really helps ensure that your tank and specimens will be healthy and get off to a good start. Exactly the same steps apply to the last freshwater dip as the first one, except that formalin is not necessary. I simply dip them for two to four minutes and introduce them directly into their new home. No further acclimation is needed because the parameters in your display tank and the holding tank should be the same, since the water in the holding tank water was taken from their permanent home. You may want to double-check the temperature to make sure and adjust it if needed.

If you have any fry in the holding tank, I would scoop them out into a smaller container and perform a series of gradual water exchanges between their holding tank water and their permanent tank. When at least half of the water has been exchanged, immerse the container in your display tank and release the young in their new home.

The final and most enjoyable step is to sit back and admire your seahorses as they explore their new surroundings. You may want to add some brine shrimp and let your herd graze at their leisure while checking out their home. Seahorses are very addictive and provide endless entertainment with their fascinating behavior and antics.

Emergencies During Acclimation

For the most part, your adult seahorses will arrive on schedule exactly as ordered and you can continue smoothly through the acclimation steps outlined above. However, any time you are receiving live specimens through the mail, the unexpected can and will happen. There are a number of emergency situations that can arise, and the hobbyist must be prepared to deal with them quickly and efficiently, as described below.

BIRTH DURING TRANSPORT

For instance, if you open your box and find you have received about 30 seahorses when you only ordered six, this means that one of your males gave birth en route. Hopefully, all of the newborns will be alive and you can scoop them out of the bag or use a turkey baster to transfer them to the acclimating container. It's a delicate task and easier said than done, but do not panic—help is here, and I'll walk you through it.

Seahorse fry are a bit more fragile than adults and cannot be exposed to air, so when transferring the fry it is best not to pour

them into the container, since there is just too much risk that some will be left stranded in the bag where they will gulp air with fatal consequences or be banged about by the torrent of water. Many of the fry will no doubt be clinging to the adults. The best way to approach this problem is to dip out the adults, tiny hitchhikers and all, with a plastic scoop (plastic measuring spoons from the kitchen work well for this) or to use a turkey baster to delicately suck up the fry. You also can attempt to very carefully pour the contents of the shipping bag into their acclimating container after first adding a little of their tank water to the bottom of the container to cushion the downpour and protect the fry. Yes, this is a tricky maneuver.

Here is a fine example of two captive bred males of two different color varieties. Note their babies all around them!

Once you have all the seahorses safely in the acclimation container, you can proceed with the freshwater dip as usual. Do not, however, dip the newborns! They have already been through quite an ordeal and are still facing an uphill struggle, so you don't want to subject them to the added stress of a freshwater dip. At this early stage in life they may not tolerate dipping well, and having just emerged from the cozy confines of their father's incubation pouch, they are already free of parasites.

You must first disentangle the adults from their tiny hitchhikers. You can remove the babies from the adults by gently tapping the newborns' tails; seahorses really do not like this sensation and will generally respond by releasing whatever they are grasping. Once you've ever so delicately dislodged the fry, you can dip the adults as usual.

The best way to deal with the fry in the acclimating container is to remove most of the water and replace it with a small quantity of water from the holding tank. Every few minutes, discard more of the water in the acclimating container and add more holding tank water in its place. The idea is to get rid of as much of the shipping water as possible. When you're confident this has been accomplished, you can take the acclimating container and slowly immerse it in their holding tank. I generally treat the holding tank with a small dose of formalin. However, this is just an added precaution and I only add the formalin on the third and final day of isolation in the holding tank.

It is a common sight to see dwarf seahorses surrounded by babies.

Birth During Acclimation

Finally, another emergency situation is having a pregnant male give birth while in the acclimation container or holding tank. This is a surprisingly common development since dwarf males are pretty much pregnant nonstop throughout the breeding season. Any time you order several pairs of dwarf seahorses between the months of February and October, you are pretty much guaranteed that at least a couple of the males will be pregnant when they arrive.

If that happens to you, and fry are being born in the acclimation container, skip the freshwater dip and move the gravid seahorse into the holding tank right away. In his delicate condition, you don't want to expose the expectant stallion to any more stress than absolutely necessary.

From the moment they are born, baby seahorses are strictly on their own, and this snow-white female feels no maternal instincts toward the newborn at which she is staring with such apparent curiosity.

The telltale signs of a seahorse in labor are repeated scrunching or jackknifing of its body and the aperture of the pouch gaping open. Labor pains are obvious as series after series of gut-wrenching spasms will wrack the seahorse's little body. As the seahorse struggles to expel the young from its brood pouch, it seems to be experiencing painful cramps that cause it to double up in apparent agony again and again. More symptoms of impending birth are described later in the section on breeding and rearing. Don't be overly alarmed. It may look like your seahorse is having convulsions, but giving birth is a perfectly normal process and I've never lost a pregnant male during delivery.

Dead on Arrival

The next emergency situation is when the seahorses are dead on arrival. Most companies that sell dwarf seahorses will offer a live guarantee, and although DOAs are rarities, it is important that the hobbyist understands the terms of that guarantee. For

example, there are a few places that require you to return the unopened shipping bag containing the specimens in the event of a DOA. This policy puts the hobbyist in a horrible quandary because dwarf seahorses are so hardy that when there is a fatality en route it is usually an isolated incident involving a single specimen, with the rest of the seahorses remaining perfectly healthy. There are likely to be several healthy seahorses in the shipping bag along with one deceased specimen, yet the hobbyist is not allowed to retrieve the lively dwarves and return only the dead individual! Essentially, you are left with the dismal choice of pocketing the loss or shipping *all* of the seahorses back, knowing full well that the healthy ones will never survive the roundtrip in rapidly deteriorating water quality due to the presence of a dead fish decaying in the bag. Personally, I feel such DOA policies are cruel and unfair.

When confronted with this dilemma, I feel the best thing to do is remove the expired seahorse and either discard it or dry it out to preserve the body. This at least allows you to rescue the healthy seahorses. Sad situations like this can be expected whenever you acquire any live creature, and it is natural to experience frustration or emotional distress over your loss.

Foods & Feeding Your Dwarves

5

Feeding Tips & Techniques

Now that your seahorses have settled into their new home, you are going to have to feed them. The first thing you'll notice is that they literally "eat like a horse!" It's amazing that such dainty, delicate-looking, little creatures can have such endless appetites. Feeding twice a day is generally best, but as you become familiar with your seahorses you may need to feed more. If their bellies start to look concave, it means they need more frequent feedings. They should have a slightly rounded belly at all times.

As of now, the most convenient food to feed your seahorses is baby brine shrimp (*Artemia salina* and closely related species), which you simply hatch at home. Hatching methods are discussed in another section. The right amount of *Artemia* to add at each feeding varies depending on how many dwarves you have and the size of their tank. A larger tank requires a heavier

Here a white striped female leans over to snick up a baby brine shrimp.

feeding in order to concentrate the brine shrimp nauplii enough to allow the dwarves to eat efficiently. Remember, dwarves are rather sedentary; they do not swim around much and prefer to wait until the food passes right under their snouts. About the most they're willing to move when feeding is to glide from one branch to another in search of greener pastures if it appears more brine shrimp are concentrated in the new location, and even this modest migration depends on the seahorse. If you have a dwarf that has a favorite resting place, then even this small effort is typically beyond its resolve.

FEEDING OBSERVATIONS

Watching your dwarves eat is fascinating. They track their prey visually with fierce intensity, draw a bead on their intended victim, and snick it up with their slurp-gun snouts quicker than the eye can follow the instant it comes within reach. When it comes to filling their bellies, they are accomplished acrobats. Dwarf seahorses sometimes dangle upside down from their prehensile tails to get at brine shrimp passing below them or stretch out full length to the very tips of their tails in order to grab prey at the limits of their reach. They will swivel almost 360 degrees to stay with a corkscrewing brine shrimp without releasing their grip on their hitching post and generally put on a pretty good contortionist act to get at fast-moving prey, all without budging from their favorite perch. Do yourself a favor and take a few minutes to enjoy the show at feeding time.

Live Foods
BABY BRINE SHRIMP

Considering the limitations of other types of food, baby brine shrimp will probably end up being the everyday diet of your ponies. Dwarves do well with *Artemia* nauplii (newly hatched brine shrimp) as their staple diet, and some will even eat adult brine shrimp, but this depends on the seahorse. The adult brine shrimp actually is not too big for them to eat, but for some reason most dwarves do not show much interest in the larger size morsels. They still seem to prefer the baby brine shrimp.

Luckily enough, a steady diet of baby brine is sufficient for seahorses, though an occasional enriching of brine shrimp that are older than three days is also a good option. There are many types of enrichment formulas you can use to fortify brine shrimp. One of the best ways is by feeding the brine shrimp with a concentrated algae paste. Just mix a drop in a little water and add it to their enriching container. I enrich in a small container and allow the brine shrimp to feast on the microalgae in it for at least eight hours before offering them to my seahorses. This is often referred to as "gut loading" the brine shrimp. As they consume the microalgae over this eight-hour period, the nutritional value of the brine shrimp greatly increases. When it is time to feed them to your seahorses, you can collect the enriched shrimp with a turkey baster and squirt them into a brine shrimp net, rinse with fresh water, and then swish the net in your tank to release the fortified shrimp.

Brine shrimp are attracted to light, so you may find it beneficial to concentrate a light source in the hatching jar/enrichment container, wait a few moments for the shrimp to congregate, and then collect them en masse.

DECAPSULATING BRINE SHRIMP EGGS

There are many successful ways to hatch brine shrimp, including store-bought hatcheries of all designs. One of these methods should be perfect for you. But before hatching out the brine shrimp eggs, I strongly advise you to decapsulate the outer shell, which is actually a protective cyst enclosing the true egg inside. This decapsulation process (or decapping for short) of dissolving away the hard outer shell may sound intimidating at first and may seem awkward when you first attempt it. However, decapping is extremely important in order to successfully feed your seahorses.

ADVANTAGES OF DECAPSULATING BRINE SHRIMP EGGS

- Reduces the risk of hydroids
- Removes the outer shell, which means less mess and no fouling of your tank
- Eliminates intestinal blockages from accidental ingestion of indigestible shells
- Kills off any and all unwanted contaminants
- Slightly quicker hatching times

Brine Shrimp Hatcheries: these are available in a number of designs, both homemade and ready-made, and 3 of the most popular models are shown here.

- Better hatch rates
- Increased nutritional value due to less energy expenditure during hatching

No doubt you will have these instructions open, your eyes glued to the page, with all of your supplies at the ready the first few times you perform this procedure. Relax; this is not difficult at all. After you've done it a couple of times, you will see how truly easy it is and realize that decapping is well worth the extra few steps. Measurements do not have to be exact but you should not overdose on the bleach. Too much bleach will destroy the eggs. Regular strength bleach is best, but ultra bleach can be used at lesser proportions. Once you decapsulate the brine shrimp eggs, you can store them for a week or more so you always have some available for hatching.

Brine Shrimp Hatchery: this is a popular commercial model designed for an upended two-liter bottle; simple yet effective.

SUPPLIES NEEDED FOR DECAPSULATING

- Brine shrimp net
- Air pump
- Plastic clip or paper clip wrapped in baggie to attach airline in the container
- Approximately 2 teaspoons of brine shrimp cysts
- Approximately 2/3 cup of bleach
- Approximately 2 cups of water

PROCEDURE

1. Pour two cups of water into a container and clip airline tubing to the side. (No air stone is needed for this.) This will keep the cysts in motion. Allow the cysts to aerate this way for approximately an hour or a little more.

2. Add a two-thirds cup of bleach—being careful not to overdose—and continue aerating. As the outer shell gradually dissolves, the eggs go through a series of color changes from brown to gray to white and finally to orange- -the color of the embryos within. This process takes about seven minutes. The decapsulation process is complete when your cysts become an orange-yellow color.

3. Pour decapsulated eggs into a brine shrimp net. Add a dechlorination product if you want, and rinse until you no longer smell bleach. This step should take about three to five minutes.

4. Drop eggs into your hatching container. You can also refrigerate eggs for about a week prior to use in a super-saturated saline solution.

While still attached to a gorgonian, this dwarf seahorse is attempting to snick up a baby brine shrimp that has come too close.

COPEPODS

Copepods are a very good food for your seahorses. They arrive in your aquarium in many different ways, and most tanks that have been established for any length of time have them. Copepods are tiny crustaceans that resemble fleas. Most hobbyists will notice them as white specks on the glass that move and hop around. Dwarf seahorses love them and will eat them whenever available, but culturing enough copepods to feed a herd of hungry dwarves would be difficult. You can seed your dwarf tank with them when you are cycling it simply by adding several copepods to your aquarium and letting them multiply naturally. You can probably get a few copepods from your local fish store if you do not have any in another tank of your own. They will reproduce pretty well. Usually, once they are planted in an aquarium, enough copepods are able to survive so that the seahorses will occasionally find one or two as a treat.

With a food source as nutritious and eagerly eaten as copepods, many people would like to culture enough of them to serve as the staple diet for their dwarf seahorses. This really would be one of the best possible food sources you could offer your dwarves, but culturing copepods in quantity can be very challenging. It would require several culture tanks running simultaneously, and collecting the breeding stock is also difficult. They just do not concentrate in swarms like brine shrimp do when you hatch the eggs. If you can possibly manage it, though, it is certainly a good idea to keep a culture or two going and offer the copepods as treats for your dwarves once a week or so.

CULTURING COPEPODS

The culturing of copepods requires them being kept in clear containers. These tiny saltwater crustaceans are very hardy. You can feed them on greenwater, which is just water that is stained greenish from countless phytoplankton (microalgae) growing in it. The copepods eat the phytoplankton, but the greenwater cultures are themselves quite prone to crashing. You also can buy concentrated forms of various algae (microalgae paste) and add that to your culture jars. Just add a drop or two of algae paste to a small amount of saltwater, stir well, and add enough of this mixture to your culture tanks to tinge the water green. Once the water starts to clear, just add more. You will want to keep the water at a very light greenish color. This will keep the copepods well fed and very healthy.

To collect the copepods you can use a turkey baster or a syringe to suck them up. The syringe method works best, but remember, this is a painstaking process and it takes time to harvest them.

CYCLOPS

Frozen *Cyclops* copepods are a possible alternative that shows some promise for dwarf seahorses. Pipefish and seahorse fry eat them well at a certain age of development, so they are worth experimenting with to see if your dwarves might like them too. *Cyclops* copepods consist of a selectively bred, biologically engineered microorganism (i.e., *Cyclops*) that is unusually rich in Highly Unsaturated Fatty Acids (HUFAs). If accepted, they would make an excellent supplement to your seahorses' staple diet of brine shrimp. (Try the frozen form only; the dried form floats on the surface and just makes a mess.)

Like Father, Like Son: an adult dwarf male stalks prey; the baby perched atop his head does the same!

RED SHRIMP

Another type of live food for your seahorses is the larval stages of larger marine crustaceans, especially the larvae of the tiny red shrimp *Halocaridina rubra* that comes from Hawaii,

The little white specks that surround this dwarf seahorse are actually baby brine shrimp. This is a good example of just how small both the seahorse and their food really is.

which you can purchase over the Internet. The adult red shrimp do not get any larger than a quarter inch, so they also make great companions for dwarf seahorses as well as a beneficial clean-up crew. Their larvae will also provide an occasional treat. These shrimp are very slow reproducers but will add a little diversity to the diet and thus contribute to the overall good health and well being of dwarf seahorses.

Other Foods
Frozen Baby Brine Shrimp

A few people have had some success coaxing dwarf seahorses to eat frozen baby brine shrimp. Unfortunately, any success with frozen baby brine shrimp seems to be fleeting and sporadic. The vast majority of dwarves won't touch them, and those that do accept them often tend to lose their taste for the frozen food quickly and unpredictably. This may be just as well,

since frozen baby brine shrimp usually deteriorate quickly and are rarely as nutritious in comparison to the live version. Consequently, I would not recommend using frozen baby brine shrimp as the staple diet for your dwarf seahorses unless you have no other options. However, this is certainly worth considering for those times when you have had a bad hatch or when live baby brine shrimp are just not handy—if your seahorses will accept them, that is. Frozen baby brine shrimp are best reserved for emergency use only, as a stopgap measure to tide you over when better dwarf foods are unavailable.

Freezing Your Own Baby Brine Shrimp

If you find that the preparation of live baby brine shrimp is hard to accomplish at the rate in which your dwarves need them, rest assured there is another option. As mentioned previously, frozen baby brine shrimp often lack essential nutrients and if fed as a staple may cause nutritional disorders in your animals. However, another option you have is to prepare your own frozen baby brine shrimp that have been enriched with various additives to give your food a boost that will allow your dwarves to thrive under aquarium conditions.

Procedure

Hatch out baby brine shrimp as previously stated, then transfer the baby brine shrimp nauplii to a holding container where they can be gut-loaded. Many types of foods can be offered to the nauplii at this time. These include but are not limited to: algae paste, *Spirolina* algae powder, green water, and bee pollen. Allow the baby brine shrimp to feed in the container for several hours. You may flood the container with food many times during the course of gut-loading as to ensure that all the baby brine shrimp will be full of the additive your offering. You may even offer multiple additives at alternating intervals to broaden their nutritional diversity. Be as creative as you wish when it comes to this practice.

After you have stuffed your batch of baby brine shrimp, it is time to separate them from the holding container and place them in freshwater to prepare for freezing. The easiest way to do this is by placing a bright light over the baby brine shrimp. This attracts them to the surface, leaving any extra egg cases and detritus close to the bottom.

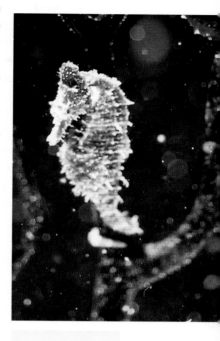

Using a brine shrimp net, available at local aquarium shops, you can scoop up large concentrations of the live, gut-loaded baby brine shrimp. Empty the contents into a container with freshwater. Continue to add baby brine shrimp until the water becomes thick with them. At this time, you may want to begin adding the slurry into small packages for freezing. A turkey baster works very well for this task. If you will be using large amounts of frozen baby brine shrimp, then ice cube trays may be what you want as the cubes of frozen baby brine can be popped out and thawed whenever needed. Ice cube trays come in several sizes, but even the smallest ones will hold more food than what you may want to thaw out at one time. In this case, fill the ice cube trays one-half or one-quarter full with the slurry. Small bags also work well, especially for more long-term storage use.

No it is not snowing in this dwarf's aquarium! Those white specks are baby brine shrimp, the dwarf's favorite food.

FEEDING FROZEN BABY BRINE SHRIMP TO YOUR DWARVES

One of the main reasons dwarf seahorses do not usually consume frozen foods is due to their lack of movement. Often, dwarves will wait for the food to come to them as they sit and wait on their hitching posts, always on the lookout for a tasty snack. This is where you will have to get creative. You will have to find a way to get the frozen baby brine shrimp to flow past

them in such a way as to trigger a feeding response. Ironically this sounds entirely more difficult than it is.

One method that seems to work with success is the use of an eyedropper. Simply suck up some of the thawed slurry and gently release a few at a time up-current of the dwarves. The current will replace the natural swimming motion of the brine shrimp causing the dwarves to thinks it is alive. Of course you will have some dwarfs on different hitching posts and must see that they get their fair share as well. Always use caution to avoid overfeeding, as this will result in the fouling of the water and deterioration of the health of your seahorses.

Over time, (some take longer than others), they will begin to snick up the frozen baby brine shrimp. Certainly your efforts will have monumental payoffs because you will then only have to give live food to your dwarves as a treat. If prepared properly, your frozen food should meet all of the nutritional requirements that the seahorses need.

With a good, healthy diet, your dwarf seahorses will stay healthy and breed frequently. It may take a little time to properly adjust the amount of food you offer at each feeding and the number of times a day you feed them, but once you work out the optimum feeding regimen for your herd, you will be well on your way to becoming a successful seahorse hobbyist.

When Seahorses Get Sick

6

The "Horsepital" Tank

Wild seahorses can be prone to illness, usually related to stress. Although you see less of this in hardy dwarf seahorses, this does not make them immune to disease. The risk of disease greatly depends on where you get your seahorses. For instance, they may have been purchased from warehouses that have held them for weeks or more in cramped holding tanks, often with other fish of dubious health and uncertain compatibility. It is not uncommon for fish to go without food during this entire time. Then when another fish store purchases them, they travel again. This can happen several times before they finally find a permanent home, after running the gauntlet from collector to wholesaler to retailer to hobbyist. Each stop along the way increases the stress on the fish, lowers their resistance, and takes a toll on their overall health.

Your holding tank can also be used as a "horsepital" (OK, hospital if you wish) tank. Using a small aquarium that is simply furnished but livable allows you to control medications used in treating problems more easily than medicating the entire seahorse tank and its many residents. It also allows you to immediately quarantine any seahorse that is not acting correctly or is showing any signs of illness. Keep the hospital tank set up and active at all times so it can be called into service at an instant.

Signs, Symptoms, and Treatments—Oh My!

When it comes to seahorses, prevention is always the best cure. Many of the most common problems that plague seahorses are associated with dirty tank conditions and poor water quality. Proper aquarium management, regular tank maintenance, and routine water changes can nip them in the bud.

Here a mandarin fish, Synchiropus splendidus, *can be seen coming out from behind a rock next to this seahorse. Mandarins are very good tank-mates for seahorses as they are usually peaceful and enjoy the same foods as well.*

Remember these are only guidelines and methods I have used myself and/or learned from others; nothing is guaranteed. When trouble breaks out, your best approach is contacting an aquarium professional or veterinarian who has experience treating fish. The Resources section in the back of this book offers information on organizations you can contact if you need help or advice.

My Seahorse is Floating

If your seahorse is a male and his pouch looks puffy, your seahorse most likely has air bubbles trapped in his pouch. This is probably the most common problem you will run into with dwarf seahorses. It is related to mating rituals and courtship displays, especially if you have equipment that produces air bubbles. As a prelude to mating, a male seahorse will often find himself playing in the bubbles while he inflates and deflates his pouch during a courtship display known as "pumping." Air bubbles can easily be drawn into the gaping pouch and be trapped as the male vigorously pumps water in and out.

The symptoms of problems with air bubbles or gas bubbles are an enlarged pouch and difficulty swimming due to positive buoyancy. Often the male will float helplessly on the surface, unable to get himself down. Without treatment this will cause a slow and painful death. Generally antibiotics are not needed to treat this condition, although a simple surgical procedure may have to be performed to remove the air bubbles. This is generally referred to as "burping" the pouch.

Burping the Pouch

The first attempt or two at performing this procedure can be very intimidating due to the small size of the patient, but after you have done it once or twice you will be a seasoned seahorse surgeon, highly skilled in burping pouches. To expel the trapped air, you will hold the seahorse with your non-dominant hand while trying to hold his tail back out of the way with a finger.

Once you have him secured, you will need something to insert into the opening of his pouch. A pouch kit purchased specifically for this purpose is the best, but you can use the coated end of a clean bobby pin or the blunt end of a toothpick or any similar clean object.

While securing the seahorse, insert the instrument with steady, even pressure, not *too* strong—we don't want to puncture the skin—but just firm enough so that the tip of the probe slips into the aperture of his pouch. He will be fighting you every inch of the way, and this is where you will need your third hand to help. Don't have a third hand? Neither do I. The first time I had to do this I sure wished I did, but after that scary first attempt, I've found this procedure to be very easy. Nowadays I can do it blindfolded, and I've even become adept at massaging the air out using only one hand.

After you have inserted the instrument into the pouch, push gently on the sides of the pouch, working from the bottom of the pouch upward to the entrance. If you are doing it correctly, you will see very tiny bubbles escape as you near the top. Push from the bottom upward a few more times until you have expelled all of the air bubbles. If all goes well, the pouch will be completely deflated and he will be able to swim completely normally again. However, if he is still floating after you release him, you will need to burp him again. This is stressful, but seahorses are very forgiving and often will swim away and start eating immediately afterward as though nothing happened.

MASSAGING THE POUCH

If this procedure sounds too alarming, there is another way of expelling the air that sometimes works and is even less invasive, called pouch massage. You may even wish to try this method first. I do not always have luck with this technique, but if it is successful, it may be easier on both you and your seahorse.

To perform this method, you hold the seahorse by your non-dominant hand and massage the pouch firmly, yet gently, working upward with a circular motion from the bottom of the tail toward the top. Sometimes with dwarves, just pressing a finger into the middle of the pouch will cause the pouch to open and the bubbles to be released. The bubbles are tiny and may spring out quickly, so pay close attention. If either operation—burping or massaging—is successful, it's an instant cure and your seahorse should be back to normal immediately.

GAS BUBBLE DISEASES

Other types of gas bubbles also commonly cause buoyancy problems for seahorses. These are collectively known as gas bubble disease (GBD), a serious condition that has a variety of causes but that is usually secondary to poor water quality or insufficient height in the tank. Tank height/water depth is generally not an issue with dwarves because of their small stature, so this is almost exclusively a concern in the greater seahorses.

There are three types of GBD that we frequently see in seahorses. One is caused by trapped air or gas buildup in the pouch (sometimes called pouch emphysema), which affects only males and is treated by burping or pouch massage, as described above.

This little guy may look like he has a swollen pouch but to the trained eye he is actually a very healthy specimen.

The second type of GBD can happen in male or female seahorses and affects their swim bladder, the small semitransparent organ located in their necks, of all places. Swim bladder problems are often associated with poor water quality, poor tank maintenance, not enough oxygen, and so on, and can be fatal.

Here a **Hippocampus** *erectus shares a tank with a banner cardinal,* Pterapogon kaudenni.

The third type of GBD manifests as superficial "blisters" that are typically first observed on the seahorse's tail. If untreated, the blisterlike subdermal gas bubbles (known as subcutaneous emphysema) can eventually spread to other parts of the seahorse's body. This condition affects both sexes and is also usually related to deteriorating water conditions.

Luckily these gas-filled blisters are almost never an issue with dwarf seahorses, and I have *never* seen a dwarf succumb to this disease. The outcome for the swim bladder and "blister" forms of GBD is often death in larger seahorses, but I have been able to treat both conditions successfully using a prolonged regimen of antibiotics.

SWIM BLADDER PROBLEMS

This complication is probably related to swim bladder problems or internal gas bubbles. It can be treated effectively depending on the overall health of the seahorse and the cause and severity of the swim bladder disorder. I recommend using 1.5 to 2 times the usual marine dose of a combination drug that incorporates a variety of broad spectrum anti-bacterial and anti-fungal agents in one product. Instructions are stated on the back of the package. The marine dose is twice the amount of the freshwater dosage, and since seahorses have a very tough exterior, I go beyond even the usual marine dosage recommended in the instructions. Treatment time can vary from a week to a month before the seahorse improves.

Badly afflicted seahorses are unlikely to survive regardless of what you try, but I have had great success using combination drugs, effective against bacterial, fungal, and protozoan infections. In severe cases, I have used neomycin sulfate in addition to combination drugs to bring about a cure. In the meantime, perform a thorough cleanup in conjunction with a 50 percent water change in your display tank.

However, take caution: neomycin sulfate and the antibiotics in combination drugs can impair your biofilter, so treatment should be administered in a hospital tank.

> ## WHAT TO DO IF YOUR SEAHORSE GETS SICK
> Of course, dwarf seahorses are subject to many other bacterial, protozoan, and viral diseases, like any other fish, as well as the usual problems due to accidents. A few of the more common—some rather dramatic—problem situations are discussed in this chapter.

ITCHING

Beware of scratching seahorses. Scratching generally means they have parasites, and although most ectoparasites can be taken care of with a simple freshwater dip, it's best not to take a chance on an infested seahorse.

Be sure to examine the seahorses' tails and the way they are hitched. If they are unable to wrap their prehensile tails completely around their hitching post, they either have a bacterial infection, a nematode problem, and/or a cut or lesion. Pass them by.

I recommend that if you observe unhealthy conditions or warning signs with any of their tank mates, do not purchase any

With invertebrates in the tank such as this orange gorgonian, you must use caution when treating any external pathogens. Many very effective treatments will kill any invertebrates in the tank such as hermit crabs or snails so be careful.

seahorses from that dealer. Unhealthy signs in a seahorse or two can put all the others at risk, and any seemingly healthy seahorses you may have been considering have likely been exposed to the same disease or parasites as well. You will be much better off getting your seahorses someplace else.

BACTERIAL INFECTIONS

It looks like my seahorse's snout is falling off or its skin is peeling off elsewhere on its body. I see exposed pink or white flesh.

The problems your seahorse may be suffering from are snout-rot (a fungal infection) and a flesh-eating bacterial infection. These hideous, disfiguring diseases are probably related to poor water quality; a superficial laceration or injury becomes infected, then secondary protozoan, bacterial, and/or fungal infection sets in and eats away the surrounding tissue (the protozoan *Costia* and *Cryptobia* are the primary suspects). Fortunately, such problems seem to be quite rare in dwarf seahorses, although I once saw a dwarf reduced to the pitiful point where its snout was half gone.

Unfortunately, the prognosis for this sort of disease is poor at best. If the lesion does not look that bad, an attempt can be made to treat it with combination drugs along with a topical ointment such as neomycin sulfate or any similar over-the-counter broad-spectrum antibiotic suitable for human use. This topical ointment can be used to treat lesions anywhere below the snout, but care must be taken not to allow the mixture to get into the fish's mouth, eyes, or gills. The prognosis is grim in severe cases, but early detection and rapid treatment can save your seahorse. The good news is that dwarf seahorses are seldom afflicted, and these pitiful diseases do not appear to be contagious.

This is a golden dwarf seahorse, one of the many attractive color patterns exhibited by this highly variable species.

Should this type of problem occur, be sure to perform a thorough cleanup of your dwarf tank in conjunction with a 50 percent water change.

EATING DISORDERS

My seahorse will not eat, and is acting funny and breathing hard. His eye movement has decreased too.

Decreased eye movement is a great early warning sign of any oncoming or present problems with seahorses. So is a loss of appetite. Seahorses are natural-born gluttons, so any time they're off their feed, it should be a major red flag for the aquarist. Diminished eye movement and lack of appetite are sure-fire signs that something is wrong in your tank, and you should immediately check your water quality and aquarium parameters.

Has there been an ammonia spike? Are your nitrites elevated? That can happen when a member of your cleanup crew dies undetected in some secluded area of the tank, or it could be an

This photo shows two of the greater seahorse species, H. kuda *and* H. erectus *hitched to a large feather duster.*

indication that your herd has now increased to the point that your aquarium has become overcrowded.

Has your specific gravity increased? What is the temperature of your tank? Is your pH off? Have your dissolved oxygen levels dropped? If any of these are off, it can stress out your seahorses. Get out your test kits and hydrometer and see if you can pinpoint the problem, then take appropriate corrective measures.

If you see that your specific gravity has increased, slowly add fresh water over a period of hours to a day or two depending on how much fresh water is needed. The optimum specific gravity is about 1.019 for dwarf seahorses. If your pH is not between 8.2 and 8.4, begin adjusting it gradually with a quality commercial buffer (avoid using baking soda for this). Nitrites as well as ammonia should be zero. A small amount of nitrates is fine, because monthly water changes usually keep nitrates within a reasonable level.

A TEMPERATURE PROBLEM

Small setups are susceptible to temperature fluctuations, and it's all too easy for the water temperature in your corral to creep above 80°F in the summer. If that happens, consider adding an extra airline or even a second sponge filter for increased aeration and water movement. You can also drop the water temperature several degrees by positioning a fan so that it blows across the surface of the water. This increases the evaporation, however, so be sure to top off your tank with fresh water daily if using a fan to cool it.

If you suspect the problem is related to water quality, then a water change will be needed, which is a very good place to start. Fifty percent water changes can be done daily until your parameters are correct. Combine your water changes with a thorough aquarium cleanup. Siphon around the bases of your rockwork and decorations, vacuum the sand or gravel, rinse your sponge filter, and administer a general system cleaning. The idea is to remove any accumulated excess organic material in the sand/gravel bed, filter media, filter sponge, etc.

If the water change(s), cleanup, and other corrective measures don't solve the problem, then it's time to seek help from a reliable source online, a good, dependable local fish store, or consult the Resources section in the back of this book for information on other organizations that can help. Aside from deteriorating water quality, various kinds of diseases can also account for the symptoms described above, and treatment will vary depending on the cause. Provide your contacts with a detailed description of the problem and they will do their best to recommend an appropriate treatment.

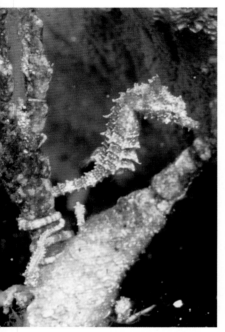

This female green colored dwarf has many white spikes covering her body. Sometimes disease is hard to notice on these specimens so daily observation is a crucial practice.

Nematodes

My seahorses are breathing rapidly, scratching, and losing the use of their prehensile tails, which have become stiff and discolored; in later stages, they became pale and emaciated and eventually assumed the dreaded "death stare." What's decimating my herd?

Your tank is infested with nematodes. Tiny parasitic nematode worms are gnawing away at the skin of your seahorses, slowly eating them alive. It is a painful, grisly business that causes the symptoms described above as it progresses.

What are Nematodes?

Roundworms or nematodes belong to the phylum Nemathelminthes and are among the most abundant animals on Earth. Though a few of the parasitic forms (such as *Ascaris* from the intestines of pigs, which you may have dissected in biology class) may be several inches long, most are minute, under one fifth of an inch long, unsegmented, and very slender white or colorless worms without an obvious head or eyes but with a distinct mouth and anus. Several thousand species live non-parasitic lives in the soil and in fresh and salt water, and several more thousand are parasites in all types of animals and even in plants. Rotifers are close relatives of nematodes, though very different in appearance.

Rapid breathing is the first symptom. Flaring gills and extremely labored breathing will signal their obvious distress. The diligent hobbyist will realize something is wrong at this point, but checking the water parameters will reveal nothing amiss.

Next, the seahorses' tails will be affected. First they will become colorless and rigid at the very tip and lose their grasping ability in that small segment of the tail. Then the

Drastic color differences in seahorses of the same species can indicate a problem. Here are two captive produced specimens of **H. zosterae.** *Notice one is far darker than the other. In this case, they are two separate color varieties but that is not always true.*

stiffness and loss of coloration will progress a little higher on the tail day by day, until the entire tail is affected, becoming a useless weight that the seahorses must drag around like an anchor when swimming. The loss of flexibility in the tail is apparently the result of the tiny worms boring into the musculature of the tail.

By this time, the seahorses will likely be scratching fiercely in an attempt to rid themselves of their voracious persecutors. If not, it's because they now lack the strength and mobility to do so. At this point, the disease will spread quickly onto the seahorse's body. Even though they are eating well, their bodies will become pale and emaciated.

Finally, the victims will lose their appetites and lapse into the "death stare." Their eyes will be fixed and unmoving, unresponsive to anything going on around them. Death is imminent and will claim them within the next day or two.

It's a slow, agonizing death, and nothing is harder than helplessly watching your prized ponies waste away like that. Fortunately, the dramatic symptoms make nematodes easy to diagnose and easy to cure.

Watch for the early symptoms described above—rapid respiration and a progressive loss of prehensility in the tail—and then confirm your diagnosis visually. Under magnification—an 8X hand-held lens is more than adequate—you can actually see the worms at work. Infested seahorses can be cleared of nematodes by using any good, commercially available, formalin-based medication according to instructions. Formalin dips and baths are very effective at eliminating nematodes.

Eradicating the parasitic worms from your tank is another matter. A relatively light infestation can be brought under control via a 50 percent water change, combined with vacuuming the substrate and a thorough tank cleanup. Serious infestations require more drastic measures. A bad nematode invasion will require moving your dwarf seahorses to a newly established aquarium, seeded with a bacterial starter to speed up the cycling process, while the infested tank is broken down and sterilized.

As with all seahorse problems, prevention is always the best

*This male is concealing himself on some **Halimeda** and liverock. Know the difference between a seahorses' favorite hitching site and when they are feeling under the weather.*

cure. Infestations of parasitic nematode worms come from the field, and they are naturally present in low levels in the aquarium. Overcrowding, dirty tank conditions, and elevated temperatures allow the nematode population to explode and build up to dangerous numbers within the confines of the aquarium. Efficient maintenance and proper tank management can help keep them in check, but the regimen of freshwater dips, formalin baths, and quarantine measures I've already prescribed for all new arrivals will assure they never get a toehold in your tank to begin with.

Odd Behavior

My male seahorse is twitching and turning colors. Is this normal?

Not to worry. The "convulsions" are actually a sign of a normal, happy seahorse with a healthy interest in reproduction. The urge to reproduce is very strong in dwarf seahorses and over-aroused males will often court their own reflections, each other, or even display to a convenient hitching post. They are just practicing, of course, getting their dance moves down for the real thing.

The Medicine Cabinet

When a seahorse is off its feed, early detection of the problem and prompt treatment are the keys to restoring its

This green male is showing a normal healthy coloration. Bacterial infections often are suspected when the seahorse is showing abnormal coloration.

health. Some diseases are fast acting, and there may not be time to make the rounds of your local fish stores searching for the right medications, much less time to order the meds you need through the mail. Therefore, it's a good idea to keep a few of the most useful medications on hand at all times so they're right there when you need them. For dwarf seahorses, you should stock your fish-room medicine chest with the following medications: combination drugs, methylene blue, neomycin sulfate, and formalin.

GRAM WHAT?

Many common disease-causing bacteria are divided into two great groups, those that react to a special stain (Gram's stain) and those that don't. If they react to the stain, they are said to be gram-positive; if not, they are gram-negative.

COMBINATION DRUGS

Combination drugs are effective against protozoans, fungus, and many kinds of bacteria. One brand that I have used with great success consists of nitrofurazone, sodium chloride, isoniazide, neomycin sulfate, and kanamycin. The nitrofurazone is an excellent antiprotozoan agent, while sodium chloride has antifungal properties. The remaining three ingredients are all antibiotics: isoniazide is a fairly decent gram-negative antibiotic, neomycin sulfate is an outstanding gram-negative antibiotic, and kanamycin is an excellent gram-positive/gram-negative antibiotic. When combined, these medications cover all the bases and the formulation acts as a particularly strong broad-spectrum antibiotic.

The only problem with combination drugs is their limited solubility. Like many medications, they do not dissolve very well in salt water. It helps if you dissolve the medication in warm fresh water before adding it to the tank. When treating with combination drugs, make sure you use the *marine* dose, which is usually double the dose on the box. Use these combo-drugs in the hospital tank only—it'll nuke your biofilter.

Combination drugs are the ultimate weapons in your medicine cabinet. They are effective against a wide range of diseases, making it a versatile shotgun for restoring order when trouble breaks out in your tank. When you suspect a bacterial infection is at work but don't know what type of bacteria is involved, don't hold back—break out the combination drugs and give the bugs both barrels!

With crystal clear water like this, why would you want to treat your sick seahorses in the main tank? It is better for your aquarium and its inhabitants if you treat sick animals in an isolation tank.

METHYLENE BLUE

Commonly known as "meth blue" or simply "blue," this is a wonderful medication for reversing the toxic effects of ammonia and nitrite poisoning (commonly known as "new tank

syndrome"). Since hospital tanks are usually without biological filtration, and ammonia and nitrite can thus build up rapidly (especially if you are not doing water changes during the treatment period), it's a good idea to add methylene blue to your hospital ward when treating sick fish.

Methylene blue also transports oxygen and aids breathing. This makes it very useful when treating gill disease, with low oxygen levels, or any time your seahorses are breathing rapidly and experiencing respiratory distress. It is the drug of choice for treating hypoxic (low oxygen) emergencies of any kind with your fish.

In addition, blue treats fungus and some bacteria and protozoans, making it another "must" for your fish-room medicine cabinet. However, be aware that it is not safe to combine methylene blue with some antibiotics, so check your medication labels closely for any possible problems before doing so.

NEOMYCIN SULFATE

Here we have a very potent gram-negative antibiotic. Most infections that plague marine fish are gram-negative, so neomycin sulfate is a super-drug for seahorses. It can even be combined with other medications for increased efficacy. Adding neomycin sulfate to other antibiotics makes a combination that packs an intense wallop for treating infections. Keep it on hand at all times. Neomycin sulfate will destroy beneficial bacteria and disrupt your biological filtration, so be sure to administer the drug in a hospital tank.

FORMALIN

This is basically a saturated 37 percent solution of formaldehyde gas in water. It is a potent external fungicide, external protozoacide, and antiparasitic, and you will be using formalin regularly to cleanse new arrivals of ectoparasites. It eradicates nematodes as well as bacteria. When used in conjunction with one of the iodine/betadine liquids, formalin makes a useful topical solution for treating external wounds and is also sometimes effective in cases of snout-rot (fungal infection) and flesh-eating bacteria (bacterial infection), if detected early.

Formalin is guaranteed to knock your biofilter for a loop, so confine its use to the horsepital—err, hospital tank—only. It also is listed as a possible carcinogen in humans, so avoid breathing its fumes and keep it off your skin. Many people react badly to contact with even small amounts of weak formalin, which may cause coughing when inhaled, sore eyes, and cracked, bleeding skin if a finger is put into the solution.

Hydroids

Those nasty hydroids in your tank look like miniature hydras for a good reason—they are closely related. These tiny animals, also related to corals and anemones, belong to the phylum Cnidaria (formerly called Coelenterata) and are recognized by the presence of tentacles and a simple digestive system with just a mouth—waste matter is regurgitated through the mouth

Tiny they may be, but the hydromedusae are armed with stinging tentacles like all jellyfish and some of them pack a heckuva wallop!

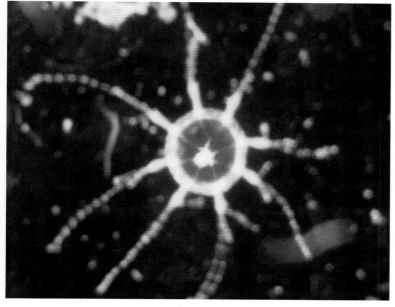

because there is no anus. Hydroids are generally colonial marine animals that form masses on all types of substrates; a few freshwater hydroids exist, and hydras are basically hydroids that have broken free of their colonial attachments with others of their kind. Most hydroids exhibit alternation of generations, the sessile (attached) polyp stage alternating with the free-swimming jellyfish-like hydromedusa stage, which swims around and allows the species to spread.

Studying the colony under high magnification, one soon becomes lost in an extraordinarily complex, living world—a microcosm in which a beautiful but deadly ballet is conducted on a microscopic scale. Hungry polyps, some resembling snapdragons, others looking more like daisies or tulips, expand their knobby, translucent tentacles, slowly flexing and languidly waving them about, lulling the observer with their slow-motion ballet—until they abruptly and quite unexpectedly snap up a bit of planktonic life, stinging it, drawing it in with one violent contraction, digesting it, and then re-expanding like a blossoming flower to hunt again. There are many such polyps in a colony, hundreds of them, each of which is armed with many tentacles and countless nematocysts, and at any given moment some of them will be dormant and still, some will be expanded and lazily casting about for prey, and others are actively feeding.

Given the right environment, hydroid colonies can overtake a tank. Unfortunately, the environment that is best for dwarf seahorses is also perfect for hydroids. In the aquarium, conditions are always ideal for them: the water temperature is always optimum, the currents are always favorable, the rich supply of food (baby brine shrimp) is inexhaustible, and predators of hydroids are nonexistent. Under such perfect conditions, hydroids can reach plague proportions in the aquarium very quickly.

To the naked eye, hydroid colonies will look similar to pinkish hair algae attached by what looks like spider webs, and if you look very closely you may be able to see the forming medusas that will eventually break off and become free-swimmers. The medusas resemble tiny jellyfish that will swim upward in a jerky, pulsating

The symptoms of a hydroid infestation can be difficult to see on dark colored dwarf seahorses.

motion and are often seen stuck onto the tank wall. They have a large "dot" in the middle of their bodies and smaller ones at the bases of their nematocysts. Removing them individually will not eradicate them.

TREATING HYDROIDS

At present, the best way to eradicate the problem is to move the seahorses to another tank. Before being transferred to their new quarters, the dwarves would first need to be quarantined for three days and then given a freshwater dip. These precautions will eliminate any hydroids the seahorses may be carrying and assure that dreaded hydroids aren't transferred to

the new tank along with them. Any remaining tank mates or items in the old aquarium need to be either left there or given a freshwater dip and moved, as applicable.

Another promising new method of getting rid of hydroids is by using a prescription de-worming agent called fenbendazole. Adding approximately 1 mg of fenbendazole per gallon of water often kills off all hydroids in their polyp and medusa stages. To use this method, remove your dwarves and any other living animals and plants and treat the tank for four days. The hydroid colonies will dissipate in about three to four days, while the free-swimming medusas may take closer to two weeks to be eradicated completely.

Adult dwarves can be safely returned to the tank after the third or fourth day of treatment. After the fourth day of treatment, you can begin removing the medication with carbon or you can just return the dwarves without pulling out the medication first.

Much work remains to be done as far as investigating the toxicity of the drug to various organisms, but it does not impair biological filtration, and the early indications are that dwarf seahorses tolerate it very well. Invertebrates, other animals, and algae are a different matter. Use this drug with care. Fenbendazole is death to all cnidarians (coelenterates); it will have dire effects on corals, polyps, gorgonians, and anemones. If you choose not to remove the medication or wait longer than four days to remove it, take that into consideration before you return the other animals to the tank. It is highly recommended that you do not add the other animals or plants until the fenbendazole has been removed and at least one 50 percent water change has been made. Again, this is a very new method of control and I have not done much research with this product, but I did have 100 percent success in eradicating my hydroid problems with fenbendazole and since then have been completely hydroid-free.

PREVENTING HYDROIDS

To help prevent hydroids from getting a foothold (tentacle-hold?) in your tank, it is crucial that you minimize the risk factors. Strict

This is a captive-bred **Hippocampus kuda** *(aka* H. taeniopterus*) in its yellow color phase.*

tank management and awareness of the many ways they can gain entry to your tank will help you reduce the possibilities of hydroid colony assaults. Hydroids are notorious hitchhikers. The colonial polyp stage or the mobile microjellies (hydromedusas) can thumb a ride on live rock, hitching posts, sand or gravel, specimens of all kinds, or within so much as a single drop of natural seawater.

When adding seahorses for the first time, or when adding new dwarves or tank mates, always quarantine your animals first. This includes plants as well. Freshwater dip dwarf seahorses and scrub the shells of snails and hermits prior to adding them to the tank after their quarantine period. If you see anything suspicious that looks like it could be hydroids attached to plants or shells, do not add them to your tank; either dispose of them or keep them separately. Snails and hermit crabs that have visible hydroid colonies attached to their shells can be lightly scrubbed and added to another tank that hydroids will not affect.

HYDROIDS AND THE GREATER SEAHORSES

Larger species of seahorses are not affected by hydroids, and once the colony's food supply (baby brine shrimp) decreases or ceases to exist, they will eventually die off. I would not take the chance of adding snails or hermits that have been "scrubbed" to the dwarf tank later on. Although you may not see any hydroids in that tank or on their shells, it is possible that they are dormant. It is best to be extra cautious, as any hobbyists who have ever experienced hydroids will tell you. It is no fun trying to get rid of them once they become entrenched. In many cases, the hobbyist is unaware that a hydroid invasion has begun until their dwarf seahorses begin dying mysteriously.

Keep all of the equipment that enters your dwarf tank separate, or use a bleach solution to sterilize any item that will be used in the tank after it has been in another aquarium. This is always good practice to prevent cross-contamination.

Hydroids may enter your tank in a number of ways. They can come in on shipments, get transferred from one tank to another by sharing equipment, and they can even enter your tank by means of brine shrimp eggs/cysts. A two-year study I performed on hydroids strongly suggested a relationship between brine shrimp eggs and hydroids. I also observed that decapsulating my brine shrimp eggs/cysts greatly reduced my chances of getting hydroids. I also found that hydroids are often associated with live rock/sand as well, particularly if it originates from Florida waters.

Reproduction

7

Courtship Displays and Rituals

The urge to reproduce is very strong in dwarf seahorses. Members of both sexes will go through the motions of courtship when there are no other seahorses in the aquarium, displaying to their own reflection in the glass or even trying to court their keeper. If no females are present, over-stimulated stallions will sometimes soothe themselves by playing in the stream of bubbles from an airstone or flirt with inanimate objects. If all else fails, the nearest hitching post will do in a pinch. Under normal circumstances, however, males have plenty of females to court, and like all seahorses, an elaborate courtship ritual precedes mating in *Hippocampus zosterae*. The courting couple will brighten in coloration, entwine tails, and dance together between bouts of more dramatic courtship displays. It's a whirlwind affair, and courtship lasts anywhere from one to three days before the actual exchange of the eggs.

The color changes that occur during courtship are usually more subdued in dwarf seahorses than those observed in the giant breeds, but I've seen brown dwarves brighten to a shade of pale, pastel pink, and lighter colors such as yellow, cream, and white are also commonly displayed as they attempt to impress each other. Metallic tints and highlights are often seen during courtship, especially on the inflated pouch of the male, and the head of the seahorse often remains dark while the rest of its body brightens.

Aside from brightening, courting seahorses sometimes sidle together, swim side by side holding tails (parallel promenade), and grasp the same strand of sea grass with their tails and prance around it in perfect unison, performing a graceful maneuver often called the Maypole or Carousel dance. But there are two dramatic displays that play an especially important role in the mating ritual of pigmy seahorses—an amazing, quivering dance-like display and the energetic pouch displays of the males

This photo shows a group of adult dwarves sharing a hitching post with several newborns.

COURTING DANCES

The dance moves demonstrated by the dwarves are fantastic and seldom seen among the greater seahorses. The dance begins with the pair perched together side by side, facing the same direction with their tails touching. One of them will begin to tremble until its entire body is vibrating rapidly from side to side, with its tail anchoring it firmly in place. It looks almost as if the seahorse is shuddering with passion. After a few seconds, it will suddenly stop, and its partner will pick up where it left off, answering back with the same rapid vibration of its body. When one stops quivering, the other resumes the dance, and the exchanges of trembling are traded back and forth for several minutes at a time. For obvious reasons, this courtship display is known as "reciprocal quivering," and it's an incredible sight to behold! It's an important part of pair formation and leads to the equally interesting pouch displays of the male.

POUCH DISPLAYS

The pouch display that is part of the mating ritual is called "pumping" because the male inflates his pouch like a balloon and jackknifes his body with a rapid pumping motion that forces water in and out of the brood pouch. With his pouch swollen to the bursting point, the male carries out a series of vigorous pelvic thrusts that are very similar to the contractions he goes through when giving birth. This flushing action is believed to cleanse the pouch and prepare it for a new batch of eggs as well as to release special chemicals called pheromones that stimulate the females. The hormone prolactin is assumed to be the most important of these chemical triggers.

Movements that may look like convulsions in a male dwarf seahorse could mean it is either courting a female or getting ready to deliver. Color changes and energetic pouch displays that mimic the spasmodic motions a male undergoes when giving birth are an integral part of the courtship ritual in *Hippocampus zosterae*. These "pouch displays" are performed with great vigor while the brood pouch is fully inflated with water and can be quite alarming the first time you see them. With its abdomen grossly distended, swollen up like a balloon ready to burst, the male's contortions make it look very much as if it's suffering from a severe bellyache, and I've received several emergency messages from panicked hobbyists who were convinced their courting males were having convulsions, or were in the throes of death.

Dwarf seahorses are very variable in coloration, as shown by the calico-like pattern of this captive-bred beauty.

EGG TRANSFER AND FERTILIZATION

One thing I've noticed about dwarf seahorses is that courtship often seems contagious in captivity. One couple will begin courting, then a nearby pair will start flirting, and other seahorses in the vicinity will follow their lead. Before you know it, pretty much the whole herd will be dancing and displaying. It's as though a chain reaction of courtship spreads throughout the colony, and pheromones may be the reason why. Because pheromones are spread throughout the aquarium when one pair begins courting, the chemicals may stimulate other seahorses as well, causing this chain reaction of courtship. Perhaps this helps explain why dwarf seahorses breed better in sizeable groups.

Eventually, the females respond to the pouch displays of their partners with a maneuver known as pointing. They stretch upward on the tips of their fully extended tails and tilt their heads back as though pointing to the surface, signaling their urgency to rise for the exchange of the eggs. By this time, they will have ripened their eggs (possibly triggered to do so by the hormone prolactin), and the courtship will soon lead to the mating itself.

Mating takes place when the partners push up from the bottom together for the copulatory rise. They bump bellies at the apex of their rise, and the female inserts her ovipositor into the aperture of the male's pouch transferring the eggs as the couple drifts slowly downward again. Unlike many of the greater seahorses, which have monogamous mating systems and form lasting pair bonds, dwarf seahorses are polygamous, meaning they have multiple partners. In fact, dwarf males have been reported to collect eggs from a number of different females in succession to form a single brood.

Gestation and Pregnancy

Regardless whether he gathers his clutch from one or more females, the moment the last egg is deposited safely inside his incubator pouch, the slot-like opening at the top of the male's pouch becomes sealed shut and the eggs are fertilized within. The brood pouch is very rich in blood vessels and placenta-like changes begin almost at once. The tissues lining the pouch expand like a sponge as the capillaries and blood

Another gaudy captive-bred dwarf, its yellow body adorned with elaborate black-edged white markings.

vessels swell and multiply, forming a separate compartment around each egg that implants. For the next 10-14 days, the brood pouch enfolds, nourishes, oxygenates, and protects the developing embryos in a perfect, temperature-controlled environment. Gestation lasts 10-14 days, depending on temperature and diet, and as their time draws near, males often become lethargic and secretive. Their pouch will be greatly swollen, making swimming difficult, and they tend to perch in a calm area and stay put for long periods of time.

Shortly before birth, however, the fry begin to writhe about and shake loose from the tissue lining the pouch. Having a mass of wriggling babies in your belly is evidently as uncomfortable as it

sounds because at this point, the male often begins to swim to-and-fro in an agitated manner, signaling its distress by changing color. Often they darken themselves, but sometimes they become much lighter than normal, assuming an unnatural pallor. Periodically, they will pause to anchor themselves to a hitching post in order to execute a series of pelvic thrusts. This is the same sort of behavior the seahorses exhibit while pumping during courtship, and it causes the mouth of his pouch, which had been tightly sealed, to gape open. It looks as though he is doubling up in agony from cramps, but the male is actually trying his best to expel his young. As he struggles to give birth, gut-wrenching spasms wrack his body. Following one such series of contractions, a tail will finally emerge from the aperture of the pouch. A few more pelvic thrusts, and out pops the first baby. A large brood may have up to 55 fry, but most broods consist of 3-35 babies with an average of about 18 fry per brood.

At first glance, they look like a bit of knotted thread, but they quickly gather themselves and swim off, miniature replicas of their parents. It's an amazing sight to see them erupting into existence like that, one by one. Once the young have left the protection of the male's pouch, no other parental care is provided. They are fully independent and able to look out for themselves.

Sometimes when a male is pregnant and has delivered a couple of fry, several hours or more may pass since any newborns have come out. However, I have seen this often, and in my experience it's nothing to worry about. The male may simply have a belly full of fry and deliver a few of them a day or two early. I'm only guessing at the reason for this, but I believe that sometimes a male may be carrying such a large brood that he becomes uncomfortable or senses that the rapidly growing young in his pouch need more room to develop properly, so he delivers some fry a little early. I can assure you that this is not unusual and that I have never lost a healthy male yet in the birthing process. My advice is to just watch him for the next few days, doing nothing to disturb him in the meantime. No doubt he will deliver the rest of his brood in a couple of days as though nothing unusual had happened.

Breeding Dwarf Seahorses in the Aquarium
MATING SEASON

Wild dwarf seahorses have a definite breeding season that may extend from as early as mid-February to as late as the end of October.   The very heart of their breeding season falls between March through August, and this is often when you will see most of the mating taking place in your aquarium. During this time of year, wild dwarf males are normally always pregnant. They typically breed in waters ranging from a few inches to a few feet deep and thrive in this highly changeable environment. At high tide they may have two feet of water overhead, or six hours later their grass flat may be above water, temporarily exposed to the air at the tide's lowest ebb. Yet the rising tide will find them alive and well, having survived in the wet mud and muddy pools amidst the beds of damp sea grass. Due to the influx of fresh water and the ebb and flow of the tides, they may experience changes in specific gravity ranging

On the left, a pregnant male hitches to a seahorse tree while a dwarf female looks on from her perch on a black-and-white **Murex** *shell.*

As shown here, dwarf seahorses love natural hitching posts like this colorful gorgonia, whether their preferred perch is alive or just the cured skeleton.

from 1.010 to 1.021 (15-30 ppt salinity) in a single day. Their ability to endure such conditions is a tribute to their toughness. Unlike most marine fishes, which prefer a specific gravity of 1.022-1.025, dwarf seahorses are often happier at reduced salinities and thrive at 1.016-1.019 (23-27 ppt). In fact, many hobbyists report their pigmies reproduce best at a specific gravity of 1.019-1.021 (27-30 ppt salinity).

So if you happened to purchase dwarf seahorses during the winter months and they are not breeding, chances are nothing's wrong but the calendar. Even captive-bred *H. zosterae* sometimes experience a lull in the festivities at this time of year. That's just their natural breeding cycle, the rhythm of life built into their genes.

Surprisingly, it isn't falling water temperatures that determine the breeding season of the dwarf seahorse in the wild. It is the hours of daylight that control their mating schedule. It turns out that dwarf seahorses breed best when the days are longer than

12 hours, and that reproduction grinds to a halt when the period between sunrise and sunset is less than 11 hours. This holds equally true for dwarf seahorses in the aquarium. So if you are an environmentally enlightened, energy-conscious aquarist, and you've been diligently switching off your aquarium reflector after eight to ten hours each day, that's the problem – you've literally been turning off your seahorse's breeding instincts with the flick of a switch!

IMPORTANCE OF LIGHT & TEMPERATURE

Since courtship is conducted primarily in the twilight hours just after dawn, a photoperiod of 2 hours half-light/12 hours full light/2 hours half-light/8 hours darkness is highly recommended for best results when attempting to breed *Hippocampus zosterae*. The half-light periods can be easily arranged by positioning a room lamp a short distance away from the breeding tank, and will provide your seahorses with a simulated dusk and dawn. Automatic timers for your light fixtures are extremely helpful for maintaining a daily cycle such as this.

In the dwarf seahorse's natural habitat, the water temperature can easily hit 90 degrees Fahrenheit (32 degrees Celsius) or more during summer months, but as winter sets in, they typically begin heading out to deeper water as the water temperature falls close to 74 degrees F (22-23 C). Biologists report that a few days after the first cold snap of the season (60 degrees F), they begin finding many more pregnant males than normal (Robert Brown, pers. com). It's as if the cold spell heralds the onset of winter, and the dwarves respond by rushing to get in one last brood before the breeding season ends.

So if your dwarf seahorses stop breeding during their season for no apparent reason, and you've been maintaining a constant aquarium temperature in the mid to upper 70s, try dropping your temperature several degrees over the course of a day. The falling water temp will simulate their normal seasonal fluctuation, which might just trigger a population explosion among your herd!

POPULATION DYNAMICS

Dwarf seahorses are highly successful and breed best if kept in groups. As a rule of thumb, the bigger the group, the better they breed. Although mating is possible anytime you have a male and female together, the chances of a successful pairing improve when there are more mates to choose from. It's simple math— the odds of finding a compatible partner improve with the number of prospective mates a seahorse has access to. In the ocean, it has been discovered that there are usually many more female dwarf seahorses than males in any given area (Strawn 1954; Vincent, 1990; Masonjones and Lewis, 1996), and that the gals outnumber the guys by as much as ten to one in some populations (Joanne Heuter, pers. com.). Needless to say, it's very unusual for seahorses, and this unbalanced sex ratio probably has a lot to do with the highly polygaomous nature of dwarf seahorses.

In fact, successful breeders often speak of their herd reaching

Good Broodstock: a nicely marked, female dwarf seahorse in her prime sporting an intricate color pattern consisting of green, white, and gray mottling.

"critical mass," the point at which it undergoes a spontaneous population explosion and becomes a self-sustaining colony. There is no agreement as to the critical number of dwarf seahorses needed to produce such an explosion, but the number I hear recommended most often is a breeding population of about 30 for starters. Some breeders say 10-12 adults are enough; others will tell you a minimum of 50 is best. You will have to reach your own conclusions for what works best for you.

Once your herd reaches a certain size, it will most likely continue to increase with no particular effort required on your part. As long as you provide your dwarves with clean water and plenty to eat, they will take care of the rest. They will be fruitful and multiply, births will greatly outnumber deaths, and enough of the young should survive to produce babies of their own so that the herd grows slowly but steadily. Once it reaches this point, a dwarf seahorse system has a life of its own and seems to thrive on a little benign neglect.

When you start out with a smaller group, say a few pairs or a mixed group of five to ten dwarves, they will often breed like bunnies at first, but then reproduction seems to taper off and the seahorses lose interest in mating after a while. When that happens, there is one sure cure that seldom fails to put your breeders back on the fast track: adding two or three new pairs of dwarf seahorses to the mix. Adding some fresh blood will almost always trigger a flurry of renewed courtship and breeding as the seahorses check out their prospective new mates and eagerly try new pairings.

As an added bonus, the newcomers increase the genetic diversity of your herd and help prevent inbreeding, strengthening the colony in the process. Compared to the larger breeds, dwarf seahorses are relatively inexpensive, so adding two or three new pairs every few months is a great way to reinvigorate your herd and stimulate breeding. Before you know it, that handful of dwarf seahorses you started out with will have become a thriving colony able to sustain itself indefinitely.

CONDITIONING THE ADULTS

Churning out brood after brood every couple of weeks is physically demanding on both the female and the male. Your brood stock needs to be in tip-top condition to keep up with the drain on their bodily resources. Dwarf seahorses that are receiving a marginal diet won't be able to keep up and will thus lose interest in breeding sooner or later as a result.

If you suspect this may be the problem with your dwarves, you need to start fortifying their food to set things straight. If you've been feeding them newly hatched brine shrimp without decapsulating it first, try decapping the eggs instead. The brine shrimp will have roughly twenty percent greater caloric value as a result, which can make a crucial difference for your breeders.

If you've been feeding once or twice a day, try three feedings a day instead. And make an effort to supplement their staple diet of baby brine shrimp with copepods, plankton, rotifers, and the larval stages of *Gammarus*, Mysids, ghost shrimp, and other post-larval shrimp if these alternatives are available to you.

Try offering them gut-loaded adult brine shrimp instead of the usual baby brine. Many adult dwarf seahorses will surprise you by slurping up the soft-bodied adult Artemia with ease despite their size. If your breeders go for the adult brine, it provides you with a wonderful opportunity to enhance their diet. Brine shrimp are filter feeders, so they will basically ingest whatever is suspended in the water with them. To fortify adult brine shrimp this way, just add enough of any quality enrichment product that's rich in HUFAs (highly unsaturated fatty acids) to barely tinge the water in a small container swarming with Artemia. After about 18-24 hours, the adult brine shrimp should have consumed most of the HUFA, boosting their nutritional value dramatically. The gut-loaded live brine shrimp can then be rinsed thoroughly and fed to the seahorses.

The way to a dwarf male's heart is truly through his stomach, and if you keep your ponies well fed and conditioned, you can be sure they will display a healthy appetite for reproduction as well.

In order to keep churning out brood after brood, your breeders must be well-conditioned specimens like this plump, golden-bronze dwarf male.

WHAT TO DO IF YOUR SEAHORSES AREN'T BREEDING

The reproduction of dwarf seahorses depends on a number of things, including the season of the year and environmental conditions such as day length, salinity, water temperature, and population. When conditions are favorable, they will readily reproduce, so if your dwarves aren't breeding, you can bet one or more of these factors are off. The point is that while stable conditions are what we always strive for in the aquarium, stability is not always best for breeding success.

If you have been keeping your dwarf seahorse tank at the usual specific gravity recommend for most marine tanks (1.022-

1.025), and you find your seahorses fail to breed, try dropping your specific gravity down to around 1.019 (27 ppt) over a period of about a day. This will simulate the sort of fluctuations dwarf seahorses normally experience in the wild, and the drop in salinity may be exactly what is needed to stimulate renewed interest in breeding.

Natural Born Hunter: this delicate looking, snow-white baby is actually a fierce predator, capable of devouring 3,600 brine shrimp in a single day!

Rearing Dwarf Seahorse Fry

Dwarf seahorses are widely considered the easiest species of seahorse to raise, but as with all seahorses, rearing is still a challenge and the hobbyist must be prepared for losses. Many hobbyists experience a 100 percent mortality rate, or close to that, with their first few batches of fry.

WATER QUALITY

Maintaining decent water quality is the primary problem. Once your dwarves start having fry, it is crucial to test your water for ammonia and nitrites often. Your herd is increasing and, boy—fry can *really* foul up your water. All those extra mouths mean that your filtration must be able to cope with a lot more eating and eliminating than normal. If you have a mature, well-established tank, this should not pose a problem. In a 10-gallon tank with several pairs of seahorses, a sponge filter is very effective, and given a mature tank, the increased load should not overtax your biofilter or cause any problems with your water quality. If you've had a real population boom, however—say several sizeable broods delivered within a period of a week or so—it's a good idea to add an extra sponge filter to the tank for supplemental filtration and aeration.

A 10-gallon tank can easily accommodate a second foam filter, cheap insurance against ammonia/nitrite spikes.

Make sure that you check daily for any fry that may have died and remove them as soon as possible. Undiscovered mortalities among the fry can pollute your tank quickly. This is one of the most important reasons I have for using black sand. Most of the fry are very light in color and stand out against the black sand really well, making them very noticeable. Fry, however, do not always drop to the substrate when they die. You may notice fry still clinging to their hitching posts after they have died. Watch your fry carefully. Do a head count and look at each one closely; if you see fry that are not moving and are hanging upside-down, chances are that they are dead. To check their condition, you can use the turkey baster and gently squirt the fry. If it just sort of circles around and does not move or grasp its hitching post tighter, then you can safely assume it has expired.

A black sand substrate shows off dwarf seahorses and their pale white babies very well, making it easy to do a daily head count and clean up afterwards.

Plan Ahead

If you are keeping dwarf seahorses, you are *highly* likely to have fry. Expect it and plan accordingly. Dwarves breed very well in the home aquarium, and very often you will receive a pregnant male when you purchase your seahorses. There are several ways to raise the young, but I find they do very well in the same tank as their parents without any special care. If you choose to keep them with the parents, just add more baby brine shrimp and feed three times a day. More feedings are fine; just make sure they are eating all of the baby brine shrimp they have after each feeding before adding more. It may take a few days for you to determine how much baby brine shrimp to add to the tank for best results. I usually add enough freshly hatched baby brine shrimp to give the tank a snowy appearance. No other particular care is necessary to raise the fry.

Lights

Lighting is another of the questions that many first-time breeders often ask about. What sort of photoperiod produces the best results when rearing fry? Personally, I have tried keeping the lights on 24 hours a day and have had great luck. After trying this for a while, I planned to keep the lights on 24 hours a day for the first three weeks after young were born, but I've found that's not necessary. As my herd grew, it appeared I would inevitably get to a point where I did not have young fry, so I decided to turn off the lights during the night. Nature does not take into consideration that there are fry in the oceans and that they could eat around the clock if provided with adequate lighting for 24 hours a day. With that in mind, I now keep my lights off for several hours at night when I sleep. I have not noticed any decrease in the growth rate of my fry or in their survival rate, so it appears the photoperiod is not that crucial when rearing dwarf fry. I suggest simply turning the lights off prior to going to sleep or getting a timer that will do it for you.

NURSERY TANKS

Some people prefer to separate the fry from their parents and raise them in a nursery tank, which is fine, but just make sure you have a cycled tank ready for them and plenty of newly hatched brine shrimp on hand. The nursery tank could be one to two gallons in size or even smaller. Just make sure you carefully monitor the water quality. Larger tanks provide more stability than the smaller ones, and daily water changes will most likely be required in the mini-nurseries. Keep in mind that you will be adding heavy feedings of baby brine shrimp several times a day. This can foul the water quickly if you don't stay on top of it. Small, daily water changes and a good sponge filter in the nursery should keep your fry happy and healthy.

If you choose to keep your fry in a separate nursery tank, you will have a choice of using either a bare bottom or some sort of substrate. Again this is optional. The benefit of a bare bottom is that you can easily see any fry that have expired on the bottom. You can also easily clean the bottom of any detritus or fecal pellets that may accumulate. This also helps slightly increase the volume of water, as there is no substrate to displace water. Many breeders find that daily water changes combined with siphoning the bare glass bottom clean during the water exchanges works well for them and maintains good water quality in the nursery.

The presence of cirri is a variable trait in seahorses. As shown here, some dwarves have none of the wispy growths, while others are downright shaggy!

Using a substrate has its benefits as well. Visually it is pleasing, and when deep enough it helps with the biological filtration (e.g., live sand beds and undergravel filters). An efficient biofilter reduces the need for frequent water changes in the nursery tank.

Again your preference is what matters. I often say that what works in one tank may not work in another. Everyone must find the method that best suits his or her own needs and abilities. The hobby is still new and there is still a great deal to be discovered when it comes to seahorse culture techniques and rearing protocols.

BREEDER NETS

Another method of raising fry is by containing them in a breeder net that sits inside of your main tank. I have had some good success with this method, but as a rule I release the fry by the two- to three-week stage, which is when the net starts to become dirty. Although there is water movement through the pores of the fine netting and the biofilter in the main tank prevents ammonia and nitrite spikes, detritus will stick to the netting. I find it becomes increasingly difficult to remove the buildup of waste and debris and keep the netting clean with this type of inside-the-tank nursery as the weeks go by. As a result, I find the breeder-net nursery to be useful simply for getting the newborns off to a good head start for the crucial first two or three weeks of their development, before transferring them back into the main tank to grow up alongside their parents. You can effectively clean the netting by briefly soaking it in a bleach solution between broods when it's not in use.

If you decide to use the in-tank net method, you will be adding the baby brine shrimp directly inside of the net two or three times a day. Some of the brine shrimp may escape, but most will remain inside of the net. Remember to add hitching posts. Dwarf seahorse fry are able to hitch right away. You can use plastic plants or fishing line for their holdfasts and hitching posts. Live plants may also be used, but I find that plastic plants and fishing line work best for this since they are easier to clean.

Hobbyists have come up with many variations of and different designs for the breeder-trap type of nursery that hangs inside the main tank, and each kind has its own advantages and disadvantages. All of these work reasonably well, and

The colors of dwarf seahorses brighten during courtship and breeding, often showing metallic tints and highlights like this golden-bronze beauty.

some are downright ingenious, but there's still room for lots of research and experimentation. Don't hesitate to try something new or to explore ideas of your own.

Whatever rearing method they prefer, most dwarf seahorse keepers are able to raise a portion of each brood to maturity once they gain a little experience. As your survival rates improve, your herd will grow rapidly. Before too long, it will be time to think about adding new tanks or finding good homes for your surplus sea ponies among your fellow hobbyists. Nothing is quite so satisfying or rewarding as dispersing healthy, home-grown seahorses to your admiring friends because your herd is growing too fast to keep up with comfortably.

FEEDING DWARF SEAHORSE FRY

When feeding your fry, be sure to use brine shrimp (*Artemia salina*) that are less than one day old. Brine shrimp are the most nutritional at this stage (first instar), since the larval brine shrimp (nauplii) will still have their yolk sacs. Feeding newly hatched brine shrimp allows the newborn seahorses to easily swallow their food through their tiny mouths. I say tiny mouths, but in reality dwarf seahorse fry are larger and better developed at birth than most seahorse species, and they are able to take larger prey as their first foods than just about any other newborn seahorses.

In fact, after their first week of growth, dwarf fry can eat older brine shrimp (second instar) that are larger, but you should always strive to feed them brine shrimp when the nauplii are at their most nutritious state. After the brine shrimp are older than one day, you can enrich the second-instar brine shrimp in your favorite enriching solution, but this does not need to be done with every feeding. Once they are more than a day old, the brine shrimp have depleted their yolk sacs and should be enriched before you feed them to your seahorses. Enriching the day-old *Artemia* for 12 to 24 hours before you feed them to your fry will fortify them with Highly Unsaturated Fatty Acids (HUFAs) and assure your seahorses get adequate nourishment. Therefore, when feeding your fry, always use either newly hatched brine shrimp (yolk sacs intact) or second instar brine shrimp (depleted yolk sacs) that have been enriched for 12 to 24 hours beforehand.

Prior to feeding the brine shrimp to your seahorses, make sure you rinse them off. The hatching water that the brine shrimp are kept in is dirty. I rinse with fresh water, preferably bottled water without chlorine.

Feed your horses that are under two months old three times a day. After they reach the two-month stage, they are mature enough to receive feedings twice a day or whatever feeding schedule you

A good feeding density of Artemia gives the tank a snowy look, like the shrimp swirling around this pregnant male.

normally follow. Keep in mind, though, that as your herd grows you may not get much time between new births.

Dwarf seahorse fry grow amazingly fast. They will double in size within two and a half to three weeks and reach sexual maturity after three to four months. In other words, after four months of rearing, your "babies" will be producing offspring of their own!

Alternate Aquarium Options

8

Keeping Dwarf Seahorses in Larger Aquaria

Most hobbyists, including myself, prefer to keep dwarf seahorses in small setups ranging from 2 to 10 gallons. The main reason is that it becomes increasingly difficult to maintain an adequate feeding density of newly hatched baby brine shrimp in tanks larger than 10 gallons. The freshly hatched baby brine shrimp need to be concentrated enough so that the seahorses can feed on them efficiently without expending too much energy. This is very important for the rapidly growing fry, which double in size after 17 days and reach sexual maturity in just 3 months.

Another consideration is the size of dwarf sea-horses.These exquisitely small, miniature marvels are not much larger than your thumbnail when fully grown and they can get "lost" in an aquarium of more than 10 gallons. This means that if a 20-gallon to 30-gallon aquarium were stocked

113

with several dozen Pixies (and it could easily accommodate hundreds of them), it would appear barren of life and quite empty from just a few feet away. However, there are a few definite advantages to keeping dwarves in a larger aquarium, especially for advanced breeders who want to maintain a colony of 30 or more adults. The larger volume of water gives the aquarium greater stability as far as fluctuations in temperature and overall chemistry, making it easier to maintain optimum water quality and generally giving the hobbyist a greater margin for error.

Well-fed broodstock will have abdomens that are slightly rounded or convex at all times, like this plump dwarf female.

Another benefit in using larger aquaria is that they provide the hobbyist with better filtration options. For instance, you cannot get a decent protein skimmer for a setup of five gallons or less, and power filters create way too much turbulence for dwarves in small tanks. In mini tanks, the intake tubes from power filters have a nasty habit of "eating" dwarf seahorses and sucking up all the live brine shrimp as fast as you can add it.

Because of this, many experienced dwarf seahorses' keepers handle this situation by partitioning or compartmentalizing a large aquarium. Ordinarily, they will use a perforated tank divider to separate the tank into two parts–a smaller equipment area for the filters and such, and a larger living area for the seahorses. The perforated barrier allows water to circulate freely between the areas while acting as a baffle that greatly dampens the turbulence generated on the equipment side. It is also very effective at keeping your newly hatched brine shrimp confined to the dwarves' living area, especially if the filtration side is kept darkened. Baby brine shrimp are attracted to intense light and will gather in large masses under aquarium lighting.

USING TABLE LAMPS

Many hobbyists use a gooseneck table lamp to further concentrate the brine shrimp in these larger setups. If the lamp is positioned at the end of the tank opposite the filtration area, it helps draw the baby brine shrimp away from the tank divider and filters while concentrating the baby brine shrimp in a smaller area, thus making it much easier for the dwarves to capture their prey. Here is where I generally place the best hitching posts as well.

DIVIDING YOUR TANK

With the tank divided this way, a protein skimmer, power filter with whatever mechanical and/or chemical filtration you care to provide, heater, deep, live sand bed (DLSB), ultraviolet (UV) sterilizer or other life support units can be safely operated in the equipment area without disturbing the dwarf seahorses or their babies in the living area. Bubble-emitting devices can run full blast in the equipment area without worrying that male seahorses might get bubbles trapped in their pouches during courtship displays. There's no danger that the horses might perch on the heater and get burned, and the filters, pumps, and skimmers can be roaring away on their side of the divider without worrying that they will batter the dwarfs with their outflow or inhale all your precious baby brine shrimp before your horses have

A well-fed dwarf seahorse in its prime like this bronze male produces a new brood every 2 weeks.

a chance to eat it. Meanwhile, the dwarf seahorses are living happily in a much smaller area than they would be otherwise, making it that much easier to maintain an adequate feeding density of baby brine shrimp, yet still enjoying all the benefits of the larger volume of water.

When large tanks are subdivided or compartmentalized this way, the aquarium is normally subdivided the short way, across its width, simply because that's how most commercially made tank dividers are designed. The clear plastic dividers with perforations come in several different sizes and can be modified to fit most standard fish tanks. The perforated plastic dividers are better than the screen-type of dividers, in my opinion, because the perforated plastic barriers do a better job of confining bbs on the seahorse side of the tank. In fact, if two of the perforated plastic dividers are positioned side-by-side with a small one-eighth or one-quarter inch gap between them, forming a double barrier, very little, if any, brine shrimp penetrate the equipment area. The mesh of the screen dividers allows shrimp to be drawn through the barrier more easily, and you usually have to turn the filter on the equipment side down or off during feedings to prevent this from happening.

If you are willing to give it a try, making your own tank divider is a suitable do-it-yourself project for any marine aquarist, and you can make the divider large enough to partition the tank lengthwise if you prefer. Thin sheets of perforated acrylic plastic that are three-sixteenth of an inch thick work well for this. They are available at plastic stores and hardware stores and can be cut to size. Plastic window screen is another option, and the plastic mesh sold in craft stores for needlepoint projects will also make a serviceable tank divider. The needlepoint plastic backing is available in different mesh sizes and varying degrees of stiffness.

Depending on the size of the aquarium, the tank is sometimes divided about one-third of the way from one end. This separates the aquarium into two-thirds living area and one-third equipment area. When more area is needed for filters, a deep sand bed (DSB), refugium, or whatever, the tank is usually divided into halves instead. Some hobbyists even use two perforated tank dividers to separate the tank into thirds; sometimes they keep equipment in both of the end compartments and use the middle one-third as the dwarf seahorses' living area, or sometimes they use one-third for their equipment area, one-third for the dwarves' living area, and one-third for keeping fish and/or inverts that are otherwise incompatible with dwarf seahorses. The tank divider will eventually get dirty and need to be cleaned. The simplest way to handle this is to slip another divider into place alongside the dirty one and then lift the dirty barrier out for easy cleaning.

Seahorses in the Refugium

A refugium is a second tank in connection with the main tank. It can also be used inside of the main tank. People often use a refugium to increase water volume, help stabilize pH, keep fauna, such as copepods, in a safe place so they will not be eaten, and house small crustaceans.

Subdividing a big aquarium allows dwarf seahorses like these two males to benefit from better filtration and the greater stability of a larger volume of water.

I am often asked if dwarves would do well in such a setup. The best way to answer this question is to reinforce the needs of dwarf seahorses and then compare them to the conditions in your refugium. Obviously, if your refugium can meet their special requirements then, yes—it can be a good place for dwarf seahorses.

For starters, dwarves do not do especially well in high currents. Given their small size and limited swimming ability, they will not thrive in refugia with overly brisk water movement.

Remember also that you will be providing baby brine shrimp at least twice a day. If the refugium is going to rapidly filter out all the brine shrimp, it won't be suitable for dwarf seahorses. You want the dwarves to eat up all that brine shrimp, not the filter.

You must also consider the way the water is transported to and from the main tank and the refugium. You do not want the dwarves or their fry to be sucked up, whisked away, and transported to the main tank.

It could also be risky if the main tank is connected to the refugium that has live rock, which is more than likely today. Live rock may be harboring hydroids—hidden colonies you may not know even exist until you start adding baby brine shrimp on a daily basis for your dwarf seahorses, causing a hydroid "bloom" in the refugium. Hydroids and dwarf seahorses just don't mix.

If you are able to design a modified refugium that addresses these concerns and meets their specialized needs, it could create an ideal dwarf seahorse ranch teeming with tasty tidbits. Such a project would require a great deal of ingenuity and technical expertise, but planning the perfect refugium for dwarves is just the sort of challenge reef keepers enjoy most.

The Modified Nanotank

The nanotank is best described as a small reef tank. Often these tanks are 10-gallon or smaller and seem like the perfect size for dwarf seahorses. Most are the right size, but one also needs to consider what type of corals and other critters are in these tanks. Strong lighting and currents are other issues to keep in mind as well as the live rock.

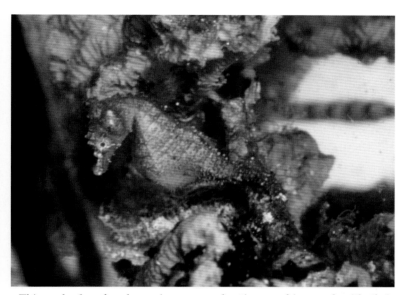

This male dwarf seahorse is a copepod-eating machine, and with their endless appetites, a herd could soon deplete the pod population in a refugium.

Dwarf seahorses are rather sedentary as a rule. They do not swim around very much, and the intense lighting required by many corals may irritate them or cause algae to grow on the dwarves. Strong currents may interfere with feeding or overpower these feeble swimmers. Some corals may sting or injure dwarves, especially the tiny fry, and many of the other critters typically found in nanoreefs (e.g., decorative shrimp, clownfish, damsels, etc.) can bother dwarf seahorses or even eat their fry. When it comes to dwarf seahorses, simplicity is usually safest.

Live rock also contains a lot of beneficial critters such as copepods that make great, healthy snacks for dwarves, but it's unrealistic to expect a nanoreef to be self-sufficient. In a matter of days, dwarf seahorses can wipe out a substantial population of copepods, and most hobbyists have herds consisting of at least three pairs. To supply several dwarves with enough copepods to eat without supplemental feedings of brine shrimp would no doubt require a huge tank.

Unfortunately, the baby brine shrimp our seahorses require are also enjoyed by hydroids. Once a colony establishes itself, you will soon have a nanotank dominated by hordes of thriving hydroids and droves of dying dwarves.

If you want to keep dwarf seahorses in a nanoreef, consider the risks and act accordingly. Use non-aggressive corals that tolerate low light-levels and lower currents. If hydroids appear, then you must be prepared to move the dwarf seahorses to a new tank. Once the brine shrimp supply is cut off, the hydroids will begin to die, but don't return the dwarves to the nanotank. As soon as you start adding the brine shrimp again, the hydroids will be back with a vengeance.

Other Captive Produced Seahorses

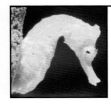

As of April 2003, there are no fewer than 18 different varieties of farm-raised seahorses available in the United States. They are comprised of 14 different species, with new phases and variations hitting the market rapidly. Many of the seahorses now available come in multiple colors and patterns, such as orange, yellow, and even a solid red. Seahorses are known for rapid color changes, depending on their mood or aquarium background; however, some of these colors are here to stay. The fixation of colors by selective breeding or line breeding is an art that has been practiced for years. Many species of fish such as koi, *Cyprinus carpio*, discus, *Symphyosodon* sp., and even the common guppy, *Poecillia reticulata,* have been dramatically altered from their wild coloration. Although the above species are freshwater fishes, the captive production of marine fishes is steadily increasing and will allow us to use these breeding techniques with them in the near future.

Color is not the only thing for which people line breed or selectively breed. Finage, or cirri in seahorses, is another trait that gives certain types of fishes their uniqueness among the assortment of other aquarium inhabitants. Many seahorses are capable of exhibiting elaborate cirri extensions in order to better blend into their backgrounds. Often, fish with elaborate fin extensions are available in a wider assortment of colors and patterns because of the many generations that are needed in order to obtain the desired results. This section of the book gives several examples of other seahorses available to hobbyists and their associated color variations.

This brilliant yellow tropical seahorse from the Caribbean is just one example of the colorful, captive-bred specimens that are now available.

A pair of Hippocampus erectus *showing the typical pattern of the Lined Seahorse. Captive-bred erectus now come in almost all the colors of the rainbow.*

Northern Seahorse or Lined Seahorse
(*HIPPOCAMPUS ERECTUS*)

Northern seahorses have been captive-bred and raised for more generations than any other seahorse, making them better adapted to aquarium conditions and life in captivity than other

seahorses. In color, they usually feature earth tones ranging from beige to brown to dark gray or black over an underlying pattern of fine parallel lines running across their chest and up their necks. But the lighter specimens that show their stripes boldly can be very striking, and they are apt to express a wide range of color phases from month to month, including everything from yellow-green to purple, to maroon and even red or orange from time to time.

These are stout, deep chested, heavy-bodied seahorses that may grow to well over 6 inches in length. Breeders select their seahorses for traits such as adaptability, vigor, disease resistance, fast growth, and greedy feeding habits—traits that increase the fitness of each line over time. After numerous generations of strengthening and improvement, the current breeds of *H. erectus* are tough as nails. Very hardy and impressive yet affordable, this species is a great choice for novice seahorse keepers who are still learning the

The normal coloration for H. erectus is a basic, earth-tone ensemble with fine, underlying lines and variable mottling.

ropes. They are very adaptable and have led the ongoing trend toward keeping captive-bred seahorses only. More than any other specimens, these are responsible for the ever-growing popularity of farm-raised seahorses.

Hippocampus erectus is available in several different colors, from yellows to reds and everything in between. The intensity of coloration is dependant on several factors: foods, aquarium background, mood, and genetic make-up. It is common for the most colorful specimens to be made up from several generations of captive—produced offspring.

Given favorable conditions, *H. erectus* can express all the glorious shades of the setting sun – yellow, gold, orange, red, lavender, lilac, and purple. Many of them are a peach color, but their coloration is quite changeable. They can be canary yellow one week, chocolate brown the next, and violet the week after that. No two specimens are exactly alike.

As this beautiful specimen demonstrates, Lined seahorses (Hippocampus erectus) *are large, solidly built, deep-chested seahorses.*

Brazilian Seahorse or Spotted Seahorse
(*HIPPOCAMPUS REIDI*)

H. reidi is the most prolific of all the giant seahorses. Famous for churning out brood after brood with relentless regularity, Brazilians hold the world record for delivering up to 2,000 young in a single brood. Not bad for a livebearer. But with that many babies crammed into one incubator pouch, the tradeoff is that the fry are born at a considerably smaller size than most seahorses. They also go through a lengthy pelagic phase, drifting freely with the plankton for weeks, making *Hippocampus reidi* fry notoriously difficult to rear in an aquarium.

The other thing that Brazilian seahorses are famous for is their intense coloration. Many aquarists consider *H. reidi* to be the most colorful of all seahorses. They can display such bold colors as yellow, orange, and red, listed in order of increasing rarity. These bright base colors are usually decorated with many small, dark spots, giving *H. reidi* one of its common nicknames—the Spotted Seahorse.

H. reidi are sleek, graceful seahorses, perfectly proportioned with slender bodies, long tails, and long snouts. Their lithe appearance gives rise to their other common names, the slender seahorse or the long-snout seahorse. If you think *H. erectus* are solidly built like a Mac truck, then long-snouts share the sleek lines of a Corvette. These are very beautiful animals and highly prized by many hobbyists.

Wild *H. reidi* are well known for their finicky eating habits, often refusing anything but certain live foods, but the captive-bred specimens thrive on a steady diet of frozen mysis. They grow slowly but are long-lived seahorses. With good care, they will be your companions for the next five to seven years and reach a length of 7 or 8 inches.

> **Hippocampus reidi,** *the Brazilian breeding machine. Large, lithe, and graceful, Brazilians are often considered the most colorful of all seahorses and captive-bred specimens like this are certainly no exception.*

Pacific Seahorse
(*Hippocampus ingens*)

Pacific seahorses are the world's largest seahorses, and these impressive animals can reach a length of 36 cm or more than 14 inches when fully grown. The prehensile tail of adults has a grip like an anaconda – giants indeed!

But for all their size, these seahorses are not at all the brutes you might imagine. They are close relatives of *Hippocampus reidi*, and share their slender profile and graceful proportions. Imagine a seahorse with the same sleek silhouette as *H. reidi*, but which reaches twice their size, and you have a pretty good picture of what Pacific seahorses are like. They are stately steeds, built like Greyhounds, which carry their size very well.

Captive-bred Pacific seahorses are a bright, golden-yellow color, overlaid with a wispy network of fine purplish lines. On closer glance, the lines begin as a string of tiny dots that merge together to form a web-like pattern of thin lines running vertically down their bodies. The fine, lilac-purple lines go very well with the yellow base color, making this an attractive seahorse.

There are several successful breeding and rearing programs worldwide for these gentle giants. This is a blessing because the wild populations of *Hippocampus ingens* are becoming increasingly threatened due to over-fishing and habitat destruction. Large, smooth-bodied seahorses in general are also much sought-after for Asian folk medicine because of their supposed curative powers for many illnesses, and *H. ingens* are especially prized due to their exceptional size. They are dried by the ton and ground into powder so they can be mixed into folk medicines and potions to treat everything from baldness to infertility.

As a result of such over-harvesting, *Hippocampus ingens*, have disappeared from large parts of their former range, leaving remnant populations scattered over a large area. Nine *H. ingens* strongholds now remain scattered from Baja, Mexico to Peru, but these isolated population pockets are at risk from habitat destruction and over-fishing.

Cape Seahorse or Knysna Seahorse
(*HIPPOCAMPUS CAPENSIS*)

Hippocampus capensis have the smallest range of any seahorse. They are found only in a few small bays and estuaries at the southernmost tip of South Africa, where coastal development has destroyed key wetlands and changed or damaged the few estuaries they depend on. They are now known only from the Knysna lagoon and the Swartvlei estuary on the cape of Africa, and their severely limited distribution puts them at great risk, making *Hippocampus capensis* the most endangered seahorse in the world.

Under normal circumstances, these rare gems would never be available to the aquarium trade, but the enormously successfully captive breeding program by dedicated aquarists has changed all that and assured the ongoing survival of this ancient species. For the first time ever, hobbyists can now keep and raise these remarkable rarities.

Hippocampus capensis *is highly endangered in the wild, but captive-breeding now assures it's survival.*

Cape seahorses are rugged, adaptable, little ponies that reach a maximum size of about 4 inches. They are large enough to be easily observed and to scarf down frozen mysis for their everyday diet, small enough to feel right at home in a small 5-to 10-gallon tank, and tough enough to thrive in water that's barely brackish or water that's twice as salty as normal seawater.

Best of all, they court and breed often, producing large, well-developed babies that hitch from birth and are relatively easy to raise. They are great little horses for aquarists who want to breed and raise their ponies or for anyone interested in keeping exotic seahorses that have never before appeared in the hobby.

Hawaiian Seahorse
(HIPPOCAMPUS FISHERI)

These are small, seagoing seahorses that prefer swimming freely in the open ocean to living in shallow beds of seagrass. They are a pacific species that are often found far offshore, and

they are very unusual because they remain pelagic all their lives.

They are small seahorses that mature at 2 to 3 inches, and yet they produce very large broods. A big, 3-inch male Hawaiian seahorse might have as many as 1,500 babies crammed into a pouch not much bigger than a thimble. That means *H. fisheri* fry are born very small (only 3-4 mm) and underdeveloped, and must spend plenty of time amidst the plankton soup catching up on their growth and development, getting scattered far and wide by tides and currents in the meantime. The end result is a small seahorse that never really grows up and settles down, even when it's fully mature, and one very much at home swimming freely in the middle of nowhere. However, they are very difficult to rear.

Hippocampus fisheri is a small, colorful, open-ocean seahorse than remains pelagic all its life.

Captive-bred *H. fisheri* can be quite colorful. Golden orange, canary yellow, red, or pink colors may be seen at times and mottled specimens are fairly common. A tank full of Hawaiian seahorses will have a lot of eye appeal, and they are a good choice for hobbyists with small setups who aren't especially interested in rearing their seahorses.

In the aquarium, *H. fisheri* do their best when offered a diet consisting of live foods such as brine shrimp, zooplankton, and mysis shrimp. As mentioned previously, they live in a pelagic state in the open ocean, and because of this, they require their aquarium water to be clean and clear. Hobbyists will often keep this species too warm. A steady temperature in the mid-70s will do just fine for this species.

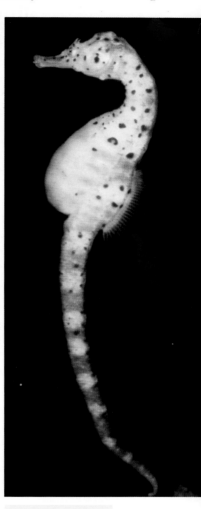

Big Bellied Seahorses
(HIPPOCAMPUS ABDOMINALIS AND H. BLEEKERI)

These big, beautiful brutes are among the largest and most massive of all seahorses and can grow to well over a foot in length (30 cm). As their common name suggests, they are deep-bodied seahorses with a very prominent abdomen, which makes them look like they have quite a belly. Males have an enormous brood pouch, which is subdivided by three to five internal membranes (other seahorses have just one). Big bellies have proportionally the longest tail and largest dorsal fin of any seahorse. This powerful propeller makes these seahorses relatively strong swimmers that range far and wide and can stand up to a fairly strong current compared to other seahorses. They often have well-developed cirri, which are frond-like extensions of the skin on their heads and necks. These tend to be more extravagant in the stallions, and male big bellies sometimes look like they're sporting a shaggy mane.

The base color of the head and body ranges from white to yellow, brown, and sometimes reddish hues. The base coloration is often overlaid with large, dark, giraffe-like spots on the head, trunk, and tail. This is a handsome, boldly marked seahorse.

The big-bellied seahorse is polygamous and males have even been known to collect eggs from more than one female to make up their broods. This is a unique trick that may be possible because their pouches are compartmentalized, allowing them to

Hippocampus abdominalis *female showing the characteristic pot belly for which this species is famous!*

Two male H. abdominalis *showing the attractive giraffe-like markings so typical of Pot Belly Seahorses.*

segregate the eggs from different females internally. Thanks to that king-sized pouch, it gives birth to the biggest babies of any seahorse (1.4-1.8 cm) and the well-developed young are fairly easy to rear despite a long pelagic period. Pregnant males give birth to an average of around 250 to 300 of these jumbo babies following a month-long gestation.

The main consideration for keeping these seahorses is that they are a temperate species that require fairly cool water. *Hippocampus abdominalis* prefer temperatures ranging from 66 to 72 degrees F (19 degrees C-22 degrees C), which requires an aquarium chiller. These South Australian giants are great seahorses for hobbyists with temperate tanks.

Sydney Seahorse or White's Seahorse
(*HIPPOCAMPUS WHITEI*)

This is another Aussie seahorse found in Sydney Harbor and New South Wales. It is a medium-sized seahorse that grows to 4 to 5 inches in length with a tall, distinctive coronet that slopes backward, a long snout, and spines above its eyes. In coloration, *Hippocampus whitei* can be brown to gray to yellowish with a sprinkling of white spots, especially around its head.

This is a promising species for breeders. The average brood size is about 100 with a gestation period of 21-25 days. The *H. whitei* fry are fairly large (8-10 mm) and easy to rear since they are able to take baby brine shrimp as their first food.

Male **Hippocampus whitei** *showing the distinctive crown and sprinkling of tiny white spots for which this medium seahorse is known.*

Short Snout Seahorse
(*HIPPOCAMPUS BREVICEPS*)

These are the smallest of all the Australian seahorses.

A pug nose and outsized brood pouch distinguish the male Short Snouted Seahorse (Hippocampus breviceps).

Hippocampus breviceps are adorable, little, pug-nosed seahorses that barely reach 3 inches in length when fully grown. They are another of the ponies that are often adorned with feathery fronds or cirri on their head and neck. Their base coloration ranges from yellowish to brown to purplish, often with a reddish tint. Many of these endearing short-headed seahorses have dark spots on their heads and striped tails.

Males have a huge pouch that is way out of proportion for their small size, and a courting male with a fully inflated brood pouch looks like a three-inch, fuzzy pipe cleaner that swallowed a golf ball! Because of their high-capacity brood pouch, pregnant males give birth to an average of 35 amazingly large babies (1.4-1.6 cm). The newborns hitch right away and are able to eat baby brine shrimp immediately.

The only drawback to *H. breviceps* is their temperature requirements. They need water temps of 66-70 degrees F, which means an aquarium with a chiller. Like dwarf seahorses, *Hippocampus breviceps* are best suited for small setups. Short snout seahorses are the perfect choice for hobbyists with small, cold-water tanks.

Zebra-Snout Seahorse or Prickly Seahorse
(*HIPPOCAMPUS BARBOURI*)

These are the pretty, prickly, tropical seahorses we all used to know and love as *Hippocampus histrix* until the taxonomists officially changed their name. The distinctive features that identify these favorites are their sharp, very well-developed spines, their prominent, five-pointed crown, and their boldly striped snouts.

Wild *Hippocampus barbouri* are pale ponies, usually white or light yellow, with reddish brown spots and lines. The captive-bred specimens are much more colorful, often a vivid canary yellow or a bright orange. Some captive-bred specimens are startling, often showing brilliant red-orange that almost hurts your eyes. The farm-raised barbs sometimes lose the striping on their snouts, but that's a small price to pay for the dazzling colors they now display.

Captive-bred *H. barbouri* are generally good breeders (polygamous), which produce modest broods (about 100 fry on average) of large fry (1.2-1.4 cm). The gestation period is two to three weeks, and when it comes to rearing, young barbs are intermediate in difficulty.

Note the prickly spines on this magnificent **Hippocampus barbouri.** *Captive-bred barbs often lose their snout stripes in favor of bold colors like these.*

Oceanic Seahorse
(HIPPOCAMPUS KUDA)

This is the Australian form of *H. kuda*, a smaller example of the kuda complex than hobbists in the USA are accustomed to keeping. The *Hippocampus kuda* that hail from Down Under (North Queensland, Northwestern Australia, Northern Territory, and Indonesia) are smaller seahorses that may reach a bit over 4 inches in length. The Aussie *H. kuda* are often black or brown but tend to be more colorful than the larger form we're used to here. Yellow, orange, and red specimens with dark brown or dark red spots are not uncommon.

They are polygamous and produce fairly big broods (about 200 fry on average) after a short, two-week gestation period. Perhaps because of their smaller size, the Australian *kuda* tend to be a little on the shy side.

Bright yellow, captive-bred **Hippocampus kuda** *showing the smooth body, undistinguished coronet, and color that make it an aquarium favorite.*

Knobby Seahorse
(*HIPPOCAMPUS TUBERCULATUS*)

Affectionately known as "tubers" by their fans, knobby seahorses are small Australian seahorses similar to *Hippocampus breviceps* in size. They top out at a bit over 3 inches but are large enough to eat small frozen mysids as their steady diet.

Hippocampus tuberculatus, of course, is famous for the raised "knobs" that it is liberally studded with, and which give it its common name of the Knobby Seahorse. They are brownish-black seahorses with reddish highlights, especially on their prominent knobs, which often stand out even the more because of their orange coloration. Male tubers have enormous brood pouches in proportion to their size, adding to their charm, and adults are often decorated with a shaggy mane of cirri. Tubers breed freely in the aquarium and produce big babies that eat newly hatched brine shrimp as their first food.

But there are two potential problems knobby seahorse keepers must be aware of. First, they are subtropical-to-temperate seahorses that do best at 66-72 degrees F (19-22 degrees C), and will be distressed if the aquarium temperature gets above 75 degrees F (24 degrees C). Secondly, they are small seahorses when fully grown, and the six-month-old sub-adults that are shipped

Knobs along the back, a shaggy mane of cirri and an oversized pouch adorn Hippocampus tuberculatus.

from the breeders in Australia are even tinier. They do best when kept in a small, grow-out tank for several months of target feeding before you transfer them to your display tank. They will do best in tanks of 10 gallons or less and need small frozen foods initially, such as the smallest brands of frozen mysis or even frozen brine shrimp.

Tropical Emperor Seahorse or High-Crowned Seahorse
(*HIPPOCAMPUS PROCERUS*)

This is a newly described species from Queensland and the Gulf of Carpenteria in Australia. It is similar to *Hippocampus whitei* in many respects, except fancier. Think of it as a tropical version of the Sydney Seahorse with brighter colors and a taller crown. It is new to the hobby but proving to be moderately easy to breed and raise, like *whitei*.

The trademark of the emperor seahorse is its exceptionally tall, backward swept coronet, which flares at the top to form a five-pointed crown. This is an eye-catching feature that makes them look like they are wearing stovepipe hats.

They range in color from white, brown, yellow, orange, red, black, or green. The vibrant yellow and red emperors are extremely attractive seahorses.

A greenish female shows the tall, backward swept coronet that is the crowning glory of the Tropical Emperor Seahorse (Hippocampus procerus).

Sad Seahorse
(HIPPOCAMPUS TRISTIS)

This is a big, beautiful, deepwater seahorse that is brand new to the hobby. It's a newly described, native Australian seahorse now being cultured by professional aquarists, and hobbyists have yet to unravel its secrets. It hasn't got a proven track record with hobbyists in the United States as of yet, so all I can say for sure right now is that *Hippocampus tristis* is one of the giant breeds, tropical, and that it shows the bright colors often seen in deep-water fishes—deep yellow to red-orange. It is a very promising, new, captive-bred beauty.

There you have it—an amazing assortment of hardy, colorful, captive-bred seahorses to consider. Besides the specimens listed above, newly developed color forms of established captive-bred lines are becoming available all the time and more new species are being raised in captivity for the first time every year. Wait until you get a load of what the seahorse farmers are coming up with next. Truly spectacular developments are already in the works, waiting right around the corner to delight hobbyists as never before.

For starters, right now aquarists are working with the *Hippocampus zebra*, by far the most beautifully marked of all the seahorses. As you might expect, they are zebra-striped seahorses with bold white stripes against a dark, red-brown background. They should be breathtaking.

New advances in aquaculture have ushered in a Golden Age for seahorse keepers, and it will be interesting to see what other new marvels the future will bring. Pretty soon we may be taking the reins on an endless supply of farm-raised syngnathids.

Resources

Online Information

The Internet is a great source of up-to-date information on seahorses, and the following websites are the best of the best. In addition to online articles and information, they feature forums where hobbyists may post seahorse-related questions and get immediate replies from the seahorse community, including accomplished aquarists, advanced breeders, and bona fide seahorse experts. They are listed in alphabetical order below.

Reef Central Online Community
http://reefcentral.com/
webmaster@reefcentral.com

With over 30,000 registered members, Reef Central is the largest and most respected hobbyist organization devoted to reef keepers. Reef Central is distinguished by an excellent online magazine that includes plenty of interesting and useful features that include a Seahorse Forum moderated by the author, Alisa Abbott.

Seahorse.org Online Community
http://www.seahorse.org/
karen@seahorse.org

Known as simply the "Org" to hobbyists, seahorse.org is the best-established online group devoted to seahorses. Excellent information on setup, feeding, breeding, rearing, tankmates, diseases and more, including a separate forum devoted solely to dwarf seahorses.

Syngnathid.org Information Exchange Board
http://www.syngnathid.org/
webmaster@syngnathid.org

Syngnathids.org is devoted primarily to seahorses, but also discusses pipefishes and seadragons, their closest relatives. This site is blessed with more than its share of knowledgeable seahorse keepers and breeders. Topping the list are the site owner/operators, Tracy and David Warland, the Wizards of Oz, who raise captive-bred seahorses for the US market at their aquafarm in Port Lincoln, Australia. Great information, again including a separate dwarf seahorse forum.

Campsen, P.J.,Paleudis, G.A., (1995). Captive Breeding and culture of the Lined Seahorse, *Hippocampus erectus*, 1995 AZA Regional Conference Proceeding, pp 528-532.

Cuen, Lucrezia. 2000. Rescuing Seahorses: Amazing Creatures Threatened by Overfishing. ABC News Internet Ventures, July 8, 2000.

Forteath, N.1996. Seahorses, *Hippocampus abdominalis*, in culture. Austasia Aquaculture. 9(6):83-84.

Forteath, N. 1997. The large bellied seahorse, *Hippocampus abdominalis*: a candidate for aquaculture. Austasia Aquaculture. 11(3):52-54.

Fritzsche, R.A. 1980. "Revision of the eastern Pacific Syngnathidae (Pisces: Syngnathiformes), including both recent and fossil forms." Proceedings of the California Academy of Sciences 42(6): 181-227.

Garrick-Maidment, Neil.1997. Seahorses: Conservation and Care. TFH Publications, Inc.: Kingdom books, UK.

Gaski, A. L. and Johnson, K. A. 1994. Prescription for extinction: endangered species and patented oriental medicines in trade. TRAFFIC USA. 300pp

Giwojna, Pete. 1990. A Step-By-Step Book About Seahorses. T.F.H. Publications, Inc.: Neptune City, New Jersey.

Giwojna, Pete. 1990. Color variations in the dwarf seahorse. Seahorse Update. 11, (5): 3-4.

IUCN. (2000). Red List of Threatened Species. [Online]. Available at: http://www.redlist.org [8 December 2000].

Kuiter,Rudie H. 2000. Seahorses, Pipefishes and Their Relatives: a Comprehensive Guide to Syngnathiformes. TMC Publishing.

Lurie, S.A.; Vincent, A.C.J.; Hall, H.J. (1999). Seahorses: an identification guide to the world's species and their conservation. Project Seahorse. London, UK.

Lunn, K.E. and Hall, H.J. 1998. Breeding and management of seahorses in aquaria: in Briefing documents for the First International Aquarium Workshop on Seahorse Husbandry, Management and Conservation, Project Seahorse. Chicago. 98pp.

Mednis, Astrida. 1998. Spreading the word about Syngnathids. Marine Education Society of Australia Conference '98 Abstracts. [Online]. Available at: http://www.mesa.edu.au/conf98/norman_m-abs.htm [8 December 2000].

Mann, Robert H. 1998. Guiding Giant Seahorses. California Wild – Academy Seahorse Project. [Online] Available at: http://www.calacademy.org/calwild/archives/seahorse.htm

Masonjones, H. D. and S. M. Lewis. 1996. Courtship behavior in the Dwarf Seahorse, *Hippocampus zosterae*. Copeia, 1996(3):634-640.

Scarratt, A.M. 1995. Techniques for raising lined seahorses (*Hippocampus erectus*). Aquarium Frontiers. 3(1):24-29.

Strawn, Kirk. 1953. A Study of the Dwarf Seahorse, *Hippocampus regulus* Ginsburg, at Cedar Key, Florida. Master of Science Thesis, University of Florida.

Strawn, Kirk. 1954. Keeping and breeding the dwarf seahorse. *Aquarium Journal* Volume 25, Number 10: pp 215-218, 227, 228.

Strawn, Kirk. 1958. Life history of the pigmy seahorse *Hippocampus zosterae* Jordan and Gilbert, at Ceder Key, Florida. Copeia, 1958:16-22.

Vincent, Amanda C.J. & Sadler, Laila M. 1995. Faithful pair bonds in wild seahorses, *Hippocampus whitei*. *Animal Behavior* 1995, 50, 3: pp 1-13.

Vincent, A.C.J. 1996. International Trade in Seahorses. Cambridge, UK. TRAFFIC International

Vincent, Amanda C.J. 1990. Reproductive Ecology of Seahorses. Ph.D. Thesis, University of Cambridge: pp 42-64.

Woods, C.M.C. 2000. Improving initial survival in cultured seahorses, *Hippocampus abdominalis*, Leeson, 1827 (Teleostei: Syngnathidae). Aquaculture. 190:377-388.

Wolf, Ben (1998). A review of the husbandry and disease problems associated with the captive culture and breeding of seahorses, *Hippocampus* species. M.Sc. Project in Applied Fish Biology. Department of Biological Sciences, University of Plymouth. Devon, UK.

Glossary

Acclimatization: compensatory change in the metabolism and physiological response of an organism exposed to temporal variation(s) in its environment.

Aerobic: occurring in the presence of oxygen.

Alkalinity: the measurement used to describe water's resistance to pH changes (its buffering capacity); also known as carbonate hardness.

Ammonia (NH₃): a chemical that is the primary nitrogen-containing end-product of protein metabolism and the breakdown of living or formerly living matter.

Anaerobic: occurring without the presence of oxygen.

Anecdotal: evidence or information based on individual example or informal case report, not from a scientific or controlled study.

Benthic: related to or occurring at the bottom of a body of water.

Captive Breeding: the propagation of organisms in aquariums or aquaculture facilities.

Caulerpa: macroscopic green marine algae often cultivated in home aquariums and very efficient at remove excess nutrients from aquarium water.

Cirrus (pl., Cirri): filament-like projections that are sometimes present on the head, nape, fins or body of some species.

Closed Systems: used to describe captive or aquarium environments that are free from natural oceanic water inputs.

Decapsulation: the process in which the shells of brine shrimp eggs are being removed in order to improve

De-nitrification: the reduction of nitrate to nitrite, ammonia, nitrous oxide, nitrogen gas, or other nitrogen-containing compounds, usually by process mediated by bacteria or algae.

Detritus: flocculent drifting material composed primarily of dead algae, coral mucus, and animal waste material and coated with bacteria and cyanobacteria.

Diurnal: active by day; occurring daily; of or pertaining to daytime.

Exsert: protruding.

Fecundity: the ability to produce large numbers of offspring successfully.

Genotype: the genetic makeup of an organism.

Genus: a taxonomic group of individuals with substantially similar characteristics and the first part of standard binomial nomenclature.

Gestation: the carrying of young in the uterus, the carrying of young in a male seahorses brood pouch.

Hitching Post: anything that a seahorse may hold onto with its prehensile tail. Gorgonians are the most common and natural form of hitching posts.

Holdfast: the specialized and flared basal portion of a gorgonian that aids in its attachment to the substrate.

Hybridization: the process of producing an organism from dissimilar parents.

Hydroid: any member of the cnidarian class Hydrozoa, but most often applied to the flowerlike polyp form of these organisms.

Macroalgae: large multicellular algae; can be red, green, or brown.

Monogamy: a mating system in which a male and female form a mating pair for an entire reproductive season or for their entire lives.

Nauplius (pl., Nauplii): the free-swimming, planktonic, larval stage of many crustaceans.

Nematocyst: the stinging structures inside the cnidocyte cells of cnidarians.

Nematodes: roundworms, any member of Phylum Nematoda.

Nitrate (NO_3): a chemical ion that is the end product of nitrification and the initial source of denitrification.

Nitrification: the aerobic process in which bacteria mediate the conversion or oxidation of ammonia into nitrite, and then nitrite to nitrate.

Nitrite (NO_2): the intermediate nitrogen-containing ion of nitrification and some forms of denitrification.

Nitrobacter: a genus of bacteria once thought to be solely responsible for the breakdown of nitrite to nitrate during biological filtration; recent research indicates other genera are also involved.

Nitrosomonous: a genus of bacteria once thought to be solely responsible for the breakdown of ammonia to nitrite; recent research indicates other genera are also involved.

Nomenclature: a system of names or terms, usually following a regular pattern of order.

pH: a measurement of the concentration of hydrogen ions in a solution; the relative acidity or alkalinity of a solution.

Pelagic: pertaining to the open sea and the organisms that inhabit it.

Phenotype: the physical characteristics expressed by a genotype.

Pheromones: chemical substances released by organisms to affect other organisms; in seahorses, little understood chemicals that are thought to be used in species recognition as involved with sexual reproduction.

Photoperiod: the duration of time during a 24-hour day in which light energy is available for photosynthesis.

Polygamy: a mating system in which a spouse of either sex may have multiple mating partners at the same time.

Quarantine: the procedure of isolating organisms in a separate area for observation and treatment before introduction into a new system; used to prevent exposure of resident populations to potential antigens, pathogens, or other problematic organisms.

Refugium: a designated or separate area within the confines of an aquarium or connected to an aquarium that allows for the proliferation of small food organisms, free from constant predation by fishes or other animals.

Species: the largest unit of reproductive capability and the fundamental individual unit of taxonomic classification.

Specific Gravity: an indirect measurement of the salinity of water, actually the ratio of the density of a given solution to the density of pure water.

Substrate: a generic term used to describe the base of an environment used to provide support or foundation. In aquarium usage, substrate may mean the sand or gravel bottom, or the rock or reef base in which seahorses can hold onto.

Taxonomy: the science or technique of classifying organisms into hierarchical groups or taxa; identifying organisms in a systematic way.

Water Column: the body of freely mobile water in a particular environment and not trapped or contained within any organism or mechanically contrived area.

Index